Michael Menichiello

A Gay Couple's Journey Through Surrogacy
Intended Fathers

D0226335

A Gay Couple's Journey Through Surrogacy

Intended Fathers

THE HAWORTH PRESS
Haworth Series in GLBT Family Studies (GLBTFS)
Jerry Bigner, PhD
Editor

A Gay Couple's Journey Through Surrogacy: Intended Fathers
by Michael Menichiello

An Introduction to GLBT Family Studies edited by Jerry J. Bigner

Titles of Related Interest:

*Fatherhood for Gay Men: An Emotional and Practical Guide
to Becoming a Gay Dad* by Kevin McGarry

*Queer Families, Common Agendas: Gay People, Lesbians,
and Family Values* edited by T. Richard Sullivan

A Gay Couple's Journey Through Surrogacy
Intended Fathers

Michael Menichiello

The Haworth Press
New York • London • Oxford

For more information on this book or to order, visit
http://www.haworthpress.com/store/product.asp?sku=5520

or call 1-800-HAWORTH (800-429-6784) in the United States and Canada
or (607) 722-5857 outside the United States and Canada

or contact orders@HaworthPress.com

The Haworth Press, Inc., 10 Alice Street, Binghamton, NY 13904-1580.

PUBLISHER'S NOTE
The development, preparation, and publication of this work has been undertaken with great care.
However, the Publisher, employees, editors, and agents of The Haworth Press are not responsible
for any errors contained herein or for consequences that may ensue from use of materials or information contained in this work. The Haworth Press is committed to the dissemination of ideas and
information according to the highest standards of intellectual freedom and the free exchange of
ideas. Statements made and opinions expressed in this publication do not necessarily reflect the
views of the Publisher, Directors, management, or staff of The Haworth Press, Inc., or an endorse-
ment by them.

Cover photo: Lillian at four months.
Cover design by Jennifer M. Gaska.

Library of Congress Cataloging-in-Publication Data

Menichiello, Michael.
A gay couple's journey through surrogacy : intended fathers / Michael Menichiello.
    p. cm.
    Includes index.
    ISBN-13: 978-0-7890-2819-8 (hc. : alk. paper)
    ISBN-10: 0-7890-2819-0 (hc. : alk. paper)
    ISBN-13: 978-0-7890-2820-4 (pbk. : alk. paper)
    ISBN-10: 0-7890-2820-4 (pbk. : alk. paper)
    1. Menichiello, Michael. 2. Gay fathers. 3. Surrogate motherhood. I. Title.

HQ76.13.M46 2005
306.874'2'08664—dc22

2005010625

To Lilly, you are my love, my joy, my soul.

ABOUT THE AUTHOR

Michael Menichiello is an award winning writer/producer. He and his partner, David, have been together for more than fifteen years and finally married in New Paltz, New York, on March 27th, 2004. Michael, David, and their daughter, Lillian, currently live in New York.

CONTENTS

Preface

When David and I set out to have a child, we didn't know what to expect because neither of us knew anything for sure. Well, that's not entirely true. One thing I did know for sure is that I didn't expect the diaries that I kept during our journey toward parenthood to be made into a book that would be published when our daughter was two years old! So, why write a book about it? Actually, I didn't write a book; I wrote a diary. I have tried to keep a journal, or diary, since I was in high school. On and off throughout my life I have started writing one and then it would fizzle out only to be started up again. I usually keep one during some drama I am having at the time so that I can write whatever thoughts, feelings, moods, or opinions come to mind and somehow it all helps after all is said and done. I started keeping another diary when David and I finally got serious about having a child. My hope was that if we were lucky enough to have a child we could share it with him or her some day and he or she could read how he or she came to be.

Tom Lorio, a friend of mine, and co-worker at the time, is the one who is actually responsible for my diaries becoming a book. So, blame him, not me, if you don't like the book! All kidding aside, Tom was the first person outside of my immediate family to know that David and I were starting the journey toward parenthood through surrogacy. Day after day, week after week, Tom would ask for "baby updates." "I hope you're writing all of this down," he said to me one day at work. "I'm keeping a diary," I said with a puzzled look on my face. "You should think about sharing your diary with other people," Tom said. "It's an amazing story." *Amazing?* I thought. *Is it really amazing?* I guess you, the reader, will have to decide that all on your own. It is what it is. It's our story. Well, it's actually our story told through my eyes. It's the good, bad, and, at times, the ugly. It's my good days and bad. It's my happiest moments and some of my saddest. It's me at my best and at my absolute worst. It's what I was thinking, feeling, wanting, hating, loving, dreading, regretting, hoping, and praying for.

I'm sharing something so deeply personal for many reasons. One is that it's the truth about our journey to become fathers. It's not *the* truth. It's *my* truth. I say it's *my* truth because it's *my* story; not everyone's. Michelle has a story of her own, as does David, and James, and everyone else involved. I told *my* truth although the names of Michelle's children have been withheld and their ages have been altered in order to help protect their identity. I also chose not to disclose the name and location of the agency we worked with as I believe that they were highly unprofessional for many reasons.

I also say that this story is *my* truth because when I first started looking into surrogacy all I seemed to find were happy stories filled with hugs, smiley faces, and happy endings. I knew that there had to be more and every once in awhile there would be a hint that things could, and did, go terribly, terribly, wrong. Part of the truth, I learned, is that some surrogate mothers regret their decisions. Every now and then I would watch how one would come forward and how she was quickly vilified and shunned by other surrogates and intended parents. No one wanted to read what they felt. Some surrogates had a change of heart during their journey—for many reasons—and would end up suing the intended parents for custody. Some intended parents neglected their surrogates and seemed to treat them very badly. All were great learning experiences, but they were rarely spoken of. I'm the kind of person that needs to know the dirt before I get myself, and my family, into something. Tell me everything; the good and especially the bad, then I can make an informed decision. But, when I asked questions about what could go wrong, or what quite often does go wrong, I was often met with a lot of resistance and a few, "why don't you get lost" type feelings. I'm also the kind of person—okay control freak—that needs to have a plan. I need to have an action plan and a response list. If A happens then I can do C, D, or E. That's how I am. But, in this case, I couldn't. As it turned out I still didn't know what to expect despite doing my homework. Maybe this book will help others see, and understand, what a surrogacy journey can be like, or was like, for someone else.

I don't want to be the poster boy for surrogacy, nor do I want to vilify it. Surrogacy isn't for everyone. In fact, David and I were very, very, lucky. I think it takes some very special people, a lot of soul searching, honesty, faith, and trust, to complete a successful journey. I also think that surrogacy, in general, should be highly regulated. As it stands, traditional surrogacy, for example, is illegal in some states, legal in others, while some state's have nothing on the books at all. This must change. I also strongly believe that agencies handling surrogacy arrangements should be legislated and that home studies should be required for both traditional and gestational agreements. The truth must also be told. I believe that children via surrogacy have a right to know how they were brought into this world. To lie, in my opinion, sets the stage for the possibility of a great deal of pain down the road for everyone involved. Lying also denotes shame and shame has no place in a loving home.

My biggest fear in sharing our journey with others isn't the impact it may have upon David or I; it's how it might affect Lilly. We still don't know how she will react to being brought into this world. We also don't know how she'll feel about having two dads, not living with her mother, having a half-brother and sister, or about anything, for that matter. But, above all else, I still wrestle with the impact this book might have upon Lilly every single day. What bothers me the most is that it's as much her story as it is ours, but she didn't have any say in whether or not it was to be shared with others. Michelle, James, David, my parents, and others, gave their permission to be included in this book, but Lilly didn't. It's a decision I might regret one day, but only time will tell. The truth is that I have no way of knowing for certain how Lilly will react or feel. She has a right to her feelings and we will deal with it as a family. Most important, we will deal with the truth.

The theme of not knowing anything for sure has followed us around since Lilly was born. A few months ago, for example, we went to dinner and left Lilly home with her babysitter. We got home and Lilly grew more and more upset as her babysitter got ready to leave. After she made her quick exit, Lilly proceeded to throw herself on the floor and scream, "Mommy, mommy, mommy!" Guilt, shame, fear, anxiety, embarrassment all started welling up inside of me. *She knows she's different,* I thought to myself. Everywhere we went if she spotted a woman she would point and shout, "Mommy!" Every time it happened I felt worse and worse. My mind raced with thoughts like, *She's only two, but she knows most other kids have a mommy and a daddy and she feels different. What have we done? She thinks everyone is her mommy because she has two daddies!* Then, about two weeks later I went to do a little grocery shopping. On my way down the produce aisle I spotted an African-American woman and her son coming toward me with their shopping wagon. As I passed by the little boy pointed at me and screamed, "Daddy, daddy, daddy!" I stopped dead in my tracks. "Why are you calling every man you see daddy?" the mom asked. "I'm really sorry," she said as she turned to me, "He's been doing that a lot lately and I don't have any idea why." "It's okay," I said. "It's really more okay than you know. My two-year-old daughter calls every woman that she sees her mommy. It's nice to know I'm not alone!" "Yeah," the mother said. "It is isn't it?" Just like that my fears were gone. Somewhat, that is. A chance happening in a grocery store ended up meaning the absolute world to me because it made me realize that I'm not alone.

Speaking of not being alone, LGBT families face tremendous uphill battles in the years to come. More and more states are filing for constitutional bans to permanently prevent LGBT people from being able to adopt, or even undergo artificial insemination, forever. It's terrifying, but it's the truth. It's a truth that we must take very seriously as once those rights are gone it's extremely difficult to regain them and they are taken away all too easily.

Hopefully this book will give people a glimpse into how difficult having a child can be for nontraditional families similar to mine. Hopefully it will also help people realize that when push comes to shove, David and I aren't any different from any other parents on the face of the earth. The only difference is that a gorgeous little girl just so happens to have two adoring fathers, not just one.

Acknowledgments

I never dreamed that I would write a book one day, let alone see it published. I owe some very special people a debt of gratitude for making it happen. First, I'd like to thank my friend, and mother of my child, Michelle, for allowing me to share our story. She didn't have to agree to it, but she did. Lord only knows why. When I originally wrote the manuscript I changed Michelle's name in order to help protect her identity, but she kept assuring me all along that I didn't have to. "I have nothing to hide and I've done nothing that I'm ashamed of," Michelle shared one day. That's one of the many reasons why I admire her so much and cherish our friendship. I'd also like to thank Michelle's husband, James. Without James' support there wouldn't be a story to tell; let alone share. I still don't know how he did it, but he did and for that I am eternally grateful.

My mother and father offered so much love, support, encouragement, and strength. I'll never forget the time we spent together in California, Mom. Never. They were some of the happiest moments of my life. Thank you for holding my hand when I was scared and for wrapping your arms around me when I broke down.

Special thanks to Richard Zmijewski for taking the photographs of David and I at our home and for allowing me to use them in this book. You truly have a gift. Thanks also to Carl Niedzielski for copyediting the manuscript for this book back in the spring of 2004. Not only did you copyedit for me, but you offered me more moral support than you'll ever know. I also offer thanks to the staff and creative team at The Haworth Press for all of their work on this project including Peg Marr, Senior Production Editor, for tactfully answering many annoying questions from this first-time author and for your expert, and witty, editing. It was a pleasure working with you and exchanging notes even if they were written in bright red pencil. Thanks also to Dawn Krisko, Senior Production Editor, for helping me with the final stages of the book and for granting me a much-needed extension! Thanks also to surrogatemothersonline.com where I first saw Michelle's ad. I also need to thank our many friends, foes, and a former friend, or two, who supported us, or made us question our sanity, and motives, during our journey. Thanks to Janine Rose, my former boss, for her help, friendship, understanding, and thoughtful advice during a long nine months when I complained sometimes more than I worked. Okay, when I complained more often than I worked. I always knew you wanted nothing more than the best for David and I on our journey and for that you have our love and appreciation. Another person that I'd like to thank is Tom Lorio. You wouldn't be reading this book if it weren't for him. Tom listened, and listened, and listened, as I explained, vented, laughed, and vented a little bit more about how hard it was to be gay and trying to have a child. Thanks, Tom, for listening and for being my friend.

There are so many other people that I should thank and I know that I've forgotten some, but please know how much your support meant to me. It wasn't easy for you I'm sure. If I wasn't the first openly gay guy you ever met I was certainly the first overly stressed out gay guy that you met who was having a child via surrogacy with a surrogate mother living 3,000 miles away. Thanks for never showing how scared to death you truly were and for never telling me how insane you thought I really was.

As for David, what can I say? I'll never forget the look on your face when you first heard me mention surrogacy. It was a mix of curiosity and you've got to be kidding me. Thank you, booger. Thank you. Thank you for standing by me for almost seventeen years, for picking me up when I fell to the ground, for never looking down on me while you stood up to support me, for always wanting the best for me, and for always wanting me to be happy. Above all, thank you for supporting me while I took the chance to be a father. Without you I wouldn't be tucking our daughter into bed at night and helping her say her, "night nights" to everyone, and everything, from the moon, and mommy, to our cat. I love you, and thank you, from the bottom of my heart.

Last, I thank God for my daughter, Lillian. Never in my wildest dreams did I ever think that I could love something as much as I love her. I truly thank God for every day that Lilly is in my life.

–1–

Baby Talk

Journal Entry, December 2001
*I just got home from a horrible day at work. First, one of my col-
leagues told me that a commercial I had just edited looked like it
belonged on a public access channel rather than a cable TV network. This coming from a woman who can't pencil her eyebrows
on straight, but she has final approval of my work? I'm just a little bitter today. Then a co-worker asked me why I had bleached
my hair platinum blond. As if that weren't bad enough, then he
proceeded to ask me whether I cared that people would think
that I was "queer." Nice day, huh? "If they don't know by now," I
said to him, "then they never will." Then I thanked him for notic-
ing. He left in disgust. Then, while sitting in horrible traffic on
the way home, I heard a news story on the radio about a surrogate mother who is carrying twins. It started out okay, I guess,
but now it's a total mess. Wow. I can't believe the things people
get themselves into. You'd think it would have scared the be-
jeezus out of me, but instead I'm completely fascinated by it.*

After almost fifteen years, David and I finally decided to get serious about having a child. We had always talked about adopting, but it
never seemed to be the right time or place: we weren't living in an
area where we would dare raise a child or we had the money but
something else took priority or we didn't have the money at all. One
of the biggest reasons why we hadn't gotten serious about having a
kid in the past was that we could never seem to justify the whole idea
of gay parenting in our own minds. We kept asking ourselves if it was
fair to the child to have two gay dads. Could he or she have a normal
life? Would his or her life be a living hell filled with endless taunting
and teasing? Would the child resent us somewhere down the line and
wish we hadn't been so selfish as to bring him or her into such a

1

mess? Was I cut out to be a parent? Would I ever stop asking myself questions?

In short, our own self-doubts were holding us back from doing anything serious about becoming parents. What troubled us more than anything was our constant worrying that a child of ours could have a normal, healthy life. In the mid-1990s we were living in upstate New York, and it was the first time in many years that we started to actually talk seriously about adopting a child. We were living in a beautiful home on two-and-a-half acres, complete with three bedrooms and an inground swimming pool. Life was pretty darn good. David and I had been together for nearly ten years, and it seemed as though we were settled. It was the perfect time to start looking into extending our family . . . or so we thought. That summer we woke up out of a dead sleep one night to hear some neighborhood teenagers screaming profanities at us. "Faggot" and "fag," along with some other choice words, were being shouted at us at two o'clock in the morning. We lived in a pretty upscale neighborhood and no one had ever given us any problems before, so we were completely taken by surprise.

The nightly tirades lasted for several weeks. Our neighbor's teenage sons pitched a tent right next to our house. Night after night I prayed for a thunder-and-lightning storm. Night after night we were woken up by their name-calling and disgusting comments. At its worst, one of the neighborhood thugs woke us up at three o'clock in the morning by standing at the end of our driveway and shining a flashlight through our bedroom window. That's when I had had enough and called the sheriff's department to file a formal complaint. We were very lucky, as it didn't take long for a sheriff's deputy to arrive at our neighbor's front door.

Weeks went by and then, lo and behold, our next-door neighbor showed up at our house with his son to apologize. I will never forget that day, for more reasons than one. We had lived next door to them for years without ever uttering as much as a word to one another, so the fact that two of them were making a beeline down our driveway was a total shock. What was also shocking was the outfit I was wearing.

"Michael!" David yelled. "They are coming down our driveway to talk to us and you're wearing your Smurf outfit! Go change your clothes!"

I was wearing a T-shirt and a pair of bright blue sweatpants. For some reason I had bought them years ago because they were on sale. I mean really, really, on sale. I thought, *Well, I'll wear them around the house and yard. No one will see me in them.* They were only three bucks or something. I was about to meet my nemesis and give him a piece of my mind while wearing my "Smurf" pants. Nice, huh? There simply was no time to change. All I could do was hope that they didn't pay attention. The first thing that teenager did after I walked out onto our deck to meet him and his father was to look down at my sweatpants. He proceeded to stand there during our entire conversation with a great big grin on his face. How could he not? Of course he denied being involved, but he did say that he was sorry for what we had been put through. "Great first impression," David said to me out of the side of his mouth after they left. Thankfully, David hadn't noticed, nor apparently had the teenager, that I was also wearing an old, and somewhat stinky, pair of bedroom slippers. It was a Friday night, after all. I was going casual.

Needless to say, that experience left us feeling that it wasn't the right time, nor was it the right place, to even think about having children.

Something always seemed to come up and we always said we'd do it next year. One year led to three years, which led to ten years, and so on.

There always seemed to be a tomorrow or an unspecified time and date when we would finally get serious and do something about becoming parents. It didn't help that every year, without fail, family and friends would bring up the subject of when we were going to adopt. Most recently, it had been the topic of a heated debate while we were at a company holiday party in 2001, in Bridgehampton, New York. A sickeningly rich, drunken married woman dressed as an elf slurred, "I don't think two guys should have kids. I mean it's just not fair to the kid. A kid needs a mommy and a daddy. Who would be a mommy if there were two daddies?" she asked, followed by a loud hiccup. Apparently what she felt a kid needed were tens of thousands of dollars of Christopher Radko ornaments; so many ornaments, in fact, that she had a special "house" built just to hold them all.

What surprised us was the fact that several other gay couples were at that very same party. Everyone, as a matter of fact, was gay except the elf, her husband, and one other colleague. However, none of the gay couples were even remotely interested in becoming parents. One couple, in particular, had been together for nearly seven years. One of them desperately wanted to have children but the other one wanted no part of it. We certainly didn't expect to find ourselves in the middle of such a heated debate.

This was on top of the terrorist attacks on September 11, 2001. It wasn't just the horror of watching the planes strike the towers; it was a feeling that all of those people got up that morning, showered, shaved, got dressed, and then headed off to work never knowing it was going to be their last day on earth. I couldn't help but wonder how many decisions they had been putting off, like we had been, or how many things they were going to do tomorrow, like we were. The fact of the matter was they didn't have a tomorrow anymore. Whatever hopes, dreams, and plans they may have had and all the things they were going to do tomorrow or next week or next year were now gone. They were gone forever.

After September 11—and to be honest, my thirty-seventh birthday had something to do with it, too—it became perfectly clear to me that if we were going to have children we shouldn't put it off until tomorrow.

Oddly enough, I never really talked to David about how serious I was. It was a matter of trying to find out as much information as I could on my own, then I would talk to him about it. It wasn't as though I came home and asked how his day was and then said, "Hey, we're gonna adopt a kid this year!" I did a little bit of research on the Internet, and made maybe one or two phone calls. Then, while on my way home from that God-awful day at work, I heard a news report on the radio about a surrogate in England who was carrying twins for a couple back here in the States. It had turned into a complete mess, because the intended parents, as they were called, didn't want twins and were insisting that the surrogate either abort one or they would put one of the children up for adoption. The surrogate ended up suing them for primary custody of the twins. I was completely fascinated, despite the fact that it should have scared the hell out of me. Needless to say, it wasn't a happy tale. I didn't know how their story would pan out at the time, but I did know that I just had to find out more about surrogacy.

On the way home—and with traffic as bad as it was that day, I had a lot of time on my hands—I kept thinking about their story. The more I thought about it, the more my head spun. I kept asking myself if these types of arrangements were becoming common. Isn't this what happened with Baby M? How do people get themselves into these messes? Were people still really doing this? If straight couples are doing this, what about gay couples?

And that's, as they say, how it all started. David and I were finally at a place in our lives where we felt comfortable enough to begin, just begin, looking into having children. It wasn't exactly the perfect time—David had just started the second half of his first year of residency in obstetrics and gynecology—but there didn't seem to be any better time to do it. It was now or never. My plan was to keep looking into adoption and keep this surrogacy thing on the back burner. Boy, was I ever in for a surprise.

I called a few adoption agencies and ordered brochures. Every time I had looked into adoption in the past I saw mountains of paperwork, unending scrutiny, not to mention that one of us would have to endure a separate stepparent adoption, and lots of waiting—waiting sometimes for more than a year, with no guarantee that we would ever have a child of our own. Overseas adoptions were being heavily advertised and promoted, with brochures making it even more enticing by saying that thousands of children were waiting for couples to adopt them. The only problem was that we didn't seem to fit the "parents" that many of these children were waiting for. Many countries listed what type or kind of parents—yes, parents—they were expecting to apply, making it perfectly clear that all applicants had to be married, and Vermont didn't count. Plus, the number of countries willing to accept applications from gay people was also becoming fewer and fewer. In addition, adopting outside of our race was something that we had long admired other couples for doing but didn't feel we could do ourselves. We felt that it would be hard enough on our child having two fathers, let alone our being of a different race.

The bottom line for us was that if we were to be parents, *good* parents, we would have to be comfortable in our own skin. Basically, if we had issues, the kid would have issues. By now it was early 2002 and we were still mulling everything over. I did more and more research on the Internet while at work—of course I did it at work; where else could I do hours of research? Most of what I found online about gay parenting dealt with adoption. I did manage to come across some Web sites that were interesting, but my search had been both frustrating and fruitless, as anytime I stumbled upon something and started reading it someone would walk up to my cubicle (or cell block, as I like to call it) and want to chat or the phone would ring. There I sat staring at my computer monitor with babies floating in clouds and ads for infertility and Viagra. So, I waited until I got home.

I honestly don't know why men take magazines into the bathroom with us, but thank God I did that night. Women don't seem to do it. It's just a man thing, I guess. Maybe it just takes us longer. Anyway, that night I happened to be reading the latest edition of *The Advocate*. I flipped through the articles and found myself looking through the advertisements in the very back. You know, the ones for companies that either can't afford or don't want a full-page ad, mostly dating services and such, but lo and behold, I stumbled upon advertisements for two different agencies that handled surrogacy arrangements for, you guessed it, gays and lesbians.

There are actually agencies that do this kind of thing? I thought to myself. *Well, at least two of them do, so there could be more.* That night and the following morning I started making phone calls and visiting their Web sites, asking them to send along brochures. As promised, two weeks later, they arrived. I was thrilled until I opened up the manila envelopes. The differences in the agencies were immediately apparent. One sent us a fancy, high-gloss, four-page, color brochure that looked like something you would get for a princess suite on an extravagant QE2 cruise, and they wanted $65,000 to $100,000 for their services. Ouch! Way out of our budget. The other sent us a folder filled with barely legible photocopied articles and notes from Kinko's, and wanted something like $50,000 plus fees—I was surprised that I didn't find a coupon in there for 10 percent off. Thanks, but no thanks!

By now, I was beginning to get discouraged. We simply couldn't afford the one, and the other wasn't much better. I didn't want a high-end Hollywood glamour baby, but I didn't want a low-end, discount bargain-shopper kid either. Plus, my mind was still spinning with questions.

That night when David came home from work, I showed him the brochures. He ended up having the same reaction as I did.

"You're really serious about this, aren't you?" he asked after a while. I wasn't sure after watching his facial expressions while he flipped through the brochures if he was as keen on the idea as I was.

However, he didn't throw them in the air with an expletive, so I thought there was at least some room for hope.

"Well," I said hesitantly, "I think it's certainly something that we should look into, don't you?"

"I guess . . ." he said. It was his only response, that night, anyway.

I knew right then and there that I had my work cut out for me. I thought that the brochures were meant to answer questions, but they led only to more questions. Why would a woman carry a child for someone else, only to give the child away? Is this legal? Is this something people actually do? Am I a desperate freak who will stop at nothing to have a child of my own? How the hell is my family going to react to this? What kind of people would do this? So, I went back to the Internet, sent more e-mails, made more telephone calls, and asked for more brochures.

> *Journal Entry, February 2002*
> *Well, I was going over the brochure from another agency last night while lying in bed and showed it to David. He doesn't seem enthused about the whole idea. I wonder why? Could it be because it's the craziest thing I've ever proposed and we don't know anyone that's ever done anything like this and it's going to cost a hundred grand? You think? It's going to take a little more time, but I think he'll come around.*

I also talked to David about it, again. "You've looked into it a lot," he said with some surprise. "I've tried," I said. "I've really tried. Are you dead set against it or should I keep looking into it?" After giving it some thought and doing some channel surfing David said, "I trust you. You've never gotten us into anything, well, too crazy before. I can't really help you with it with work and all, but if you want, I trust you. Why don't you look into it more?" If he only knew how much he would regret that statement.

It took a few more phone calls and a couple more days of researching at work to track down another agency in a nearby state. I wanted to find one close to us, as I thought then we would have a better chance of finding a surrogate that was close by, too. Well, our surrogate ended up living 3,000 miles away in Nevada! But I'm getting ahead of myself.

I e-mailed the agency for a brochure, and when it came I was pleasantly surprised that it was done simply and tastefully. I made the initial telephone call while David was working a twenty-four-hour shift, and a lot of my questions were finally answered.

For starters, no, surrogacy isn't "legal" in all states, including New York, where we live. Some states, such as California, are very lenient and actually have laws that make it quite appealing for gay couples to pursue surrogacy, while others have flat-out made it illegal to enter into a surrogate contract. Come to find out, to some courts (and even some individuals, as I would later discover), surrogacy is nothing more than "baby selling and baby buying." Isn't that wonderful? It's like going to Target, picking out a kid, and taking it up to the checkout counter to scan the bar code on the bum. The issue of baby buying and selling would come back to haunt us over and over again. We would also learn that we were looking for a traditional surrogate, rather than gestational. A *gestational* surrogate is artificially inseminated with donated sperm and a donated egg. A *traditional* surrogate donates her own egg and sperm comes from one of the intended parents. Yes, that means that she does have a biological connection with the child. The other difference was price. With a gestational surrogate we would have to find and pay for an egg donor. Then, there were weeks, if not months, of rather expensive fertility treatments. Multiples weren't uncommon either, because of the fertility drugs. So, we moved forward but still had a ton of questions. Would we be able to find someone willing to do this for a gay couple? What would we tell our child about how he or she came to be? Most, if not all, of our questions were answered one by one. It was a painstaking process.

First, the agency director assured us that they had a full roster of surrogates ready, willing, and able to help David and I become fathers. So we asked to see a contract and had it in hand with lightning speed. (That was the first and last thing our agency did with any kind of speed—more about that nightmare later on.) We were also asked to fill out a lengthy questionnaire. Our profile would be shared with a surrogate. We would then get her full profile if she expressed interest. They call this the "match" in the world of surrogacy. It took us a week or so, but we finally managed to answer all the questions in our profile.

After we signed the contract and agreed to pay $10,000 for their services, the agency gave us access to their Web site, where we could view personal profiles that surrogates had filled out and submitted. Some of the information was physical, such as height, weight, and eye color; most of it was question and answer. Questions ranged from "Why do you want to be a surrogate mother?" and "Have you had children before?" to "Would your describe your pregnancies as difficult or relatively easy?"

We were happy, but a little overwhelmed, to see that there were a dozen or so women willing to help us have a child. Out of twenty-five surrogates, about fifteen were willing to help a gay couple. They were already mothers of their own, had already completed their families, and had the full support of their spouses. They weren't the richest women in the world, nor were they the poorest. Some wanted very little compensation ($15,000 for a first-time surrogate), while other, more experienced surrogates were looking for a little more ($25,000 and up). Most had finished high school; a few had gone on to college. Ages ranged from nineteen to twenty-nine. I can't tell you how hard it was reading through all of those profiles. It felt strange and awkward, even though we weren't meeting any of them face-to-face; it still felt as though we were "selecting" someone. What gave us the right to do that? It was like a dating game or a cattle call from my acting days in New York. You were lined up, eyed up and down, then you were either asked to step forward or backward and then all you heard was someone screaming "Next!" from a black void.

"There are definitely certain things you should look for," the owner of the agency instructed us. "Ask yourself what is most important to you. Do you want a surrogate who resembles you? Do you want someone who is college educated or has some education? Should she be married or is it okay if she's single? Does she have health care? Is she employed full-time? Is she healthy? Does she live in a surrogate-friendly state?" Now my head was completely spinning, but I still had more questions. One question that kept coming back to me was why would a woman do this? Why on earth would a woman get pregnant with someone else's child, carry it to term, deliver it, and walk away? Why? How? By the end of the week we were back on the phone with the agency asking that very same question.

"I think they do it for a lot of reasons. Some enjoy being pregnant. Their pregnancies are relatively carefree," the director explained. "Sure, they have morning sickness and all, but no major complications. However, I'm sure there are those that, well, let's just say the money doesn't hurt."

I knew what he was saying. I could understand what he was saying. No one, unless she's a saint, would carry a child for you without being compensated in some way, shape, or form, right? "Some surrogates," the director continued, "don't ask for a fee. They ask that you take care of other things such as their health coverage and health-related expenses, and day care for their own children if they need to be away for a while. Others just ask for living expenses."

"Living expenses like what?" David asked.

"Oh, housekeeping, parking, extra money for food if they eat more while they are pregnant. Those kinds of things," the director rattled off.

What followed was a really, really, long pause. The kind of pause that is excruciatingly uncomfortable. Come to find out, David and I were thinking the very same thing.

"I don't mind or have a problem with compensating someone," I broke in, "or paying for living expenses, or pain and suffering, but we don't want to feel as though we are taking advantage of someone either." The bottom line for us was that we weren't going to work with a surrogate who needed money. If, for example, she had to live off of the compensation, or didn't have enought money to pay for something like parking, we wouldn't feel comfortable and would find someone else to help us. "If someone is less fortunate than us," I tried to explain, "it seems like it turns into the 'haves' versus the 'have-nots.'"

"Let's say," David finally chimed in to either bail me out or shut me up, "they want to be paid twenty thousand dollars. To us that's a lot of money. To someone else that's a small fortune. There's a difference."

"Feeling like we're taking advantage of someone would be an awful feeling," I said flatly. "I don't want to do this if we even remotely feel that we're taking advantage of someone."

"That's admirable," the director said after taking a moment to take it all in.

"We don't want to be admirable," David said, "we just want to be able to live with ourselves and be able to tell our child the truth someday without being all embarrassed or weird about it. They're going to have enough whammies against them as it is."

The director completely understood where we were coming from and said that perhaps we should make it a point to find someone who was relatively self-sufficient; someone who worked outside the home and had some means of an income.

"That would make us feel a lot better," I said, feeling relieved. "Now keep in mind," we were cautioned, "she won't be a high-powered executive making two hundred fifty thousand dollars a year, but it sounds as though it's very important to both of you that she be self-sufficient, so that's what you should look for."

"What about health care?" I asked. My health insurance would cover David, but not a surrogate mother. "Most surrogates that we work with," he explained, "have their own health coverage. It's a tremendous expense to take it out yourself, which you could do, but it's better to find someone who has existing coverage that includes surrogacy."

> *Journal Entry, March 2002*
> *I can't believe how seriously we're looking into this surrogacy idea. I thought for sure we would adopt. But this surrogacy thing seems so complicated. There are so many issues, and questions. Just when we answer one question, another one pops up. Isn't it cool that I could have a biological child of my own? I would have never dreamed of it. It seems like it could turn into a huge mess really easily, though. I just still can't believe how seriously we're looking into it.*

It took us a while, but we managed to figure out what mattered most to us. We were searching for a surrogate who resembled me; well, the platinum blond hair wasn't mandatory: it was temporary after all. I say me, because we had decided, yes, we, that I would go first. We also wanted someone who worked full-time so that she wouldn't be solely reliant on the compensation. Health coverage was a must, and we decided that we wanted to work with someone who was married, preferably to a supportive spouse. The only problem was that after going over many of the profiles, we realized that not one of the surrogates lived even remotely close to us. I put in another phone call to the agency.

"It's more important that you find a surrogate that you like," we were told, "a surrogate you feel comfortable with and with whom you feel you can work. Worry about that first."

"But," I asked, "if she lives too far away we won't be able to go to doctor's appointments and things like that. Isn't that a huge drawback?"

"Not necessarily," the director said. "It depends upon just how involved she wants you to be. Some want constant attention and want you to be present at any and all appointments, while others don't want you to be hovering over them all the time. Besides that, isn't it better to have a surrogate you like and want to work with who lives in California, rather than someone who lives in New York with whom you're having all kinds of problems?" *Good point,* I thought.

So, with all that out of the way and some of our questions answered, we could finally start to look over some more profiles. When we were really stuck, we took them with us while visiting my parents in upstate New York. My sister, Debbie, even took a peek when she popped in unexpectedly. They all agreed how strange it was to be going over profiles of total strangers to see if you would have a child with them.

"Hey," I said to break the tension in the air, "strange is par for the course when you're dealing with David and me, isn't it?"

Journal Entry, March 2002
It's three-thirty in the morning and I'm wide awake. David is snoring away. I think I'm having a panic attack. I woke up sweating, heart racing and head spinning. What am I doing? I'm talking about having a child with a total stranger. I'm actually going over profiles of strangers trying to find someone to carry my child. Am I nuts? Is this crazy? I must be crazy. It's all falling into place, though. First the news report, then the agency, then the Web site. If it's not right, then why is it all happening?

After nearly two weeks of mulling over profiles, we were finally able to narrow it down to six or seven surrogates that we were interested in and wanted to learn more about. Little did we know we weren't done yet; we were in for a total shocker. We called the agency excitedly the next morning to go over our list of surrogates, but we quickly learned that not one of the more than half a dozen surrogates we were interested in was available. Not one of them.

"How can this be?" David asked the agency.

"Most of the surrogates work with several agencies at once," they explained, "or list themselves with as many reputable agencies as they can, and some aren't very good about keeping in touch with us and letting us know if they are or aren't available."

"Now what do we do?" I asked.

"We'll go through our listings and make certain who is and who isn't available and I'll get back to you shortly," we were told convincingly.

Weeks passed before we heard anything from our agency. For all we knew they had taken off for Maui with our money in hand. So much for a lightning-fast response!

In the meantime, I got back on the Internet and started searching for a surrogate mother on my own. Yes, completely on my own. I still find it hard to believe that I actually did it. I knew absolutely nothing about what I was doing but figured that I could just find someone and then direct them to our agency. Brilliant idea, wasn't it? How hard could it be? Believe it or not, I somehow managed to stumble upon surrogatemothersonline.com, an entire Web site devoted exclusively to surrogacy. It had message boards, online advertisements, subjects broken down into categories, and just a lot of interesting stuff. I couldn't believe my eyes. It was a thriving community. I half expected to see a dozen or so crazy people, but this site had thousands of members and had been up and running for many years. I spent hours looking over the site and eventually discovered the classified section. Before I knew it, I was writing an ad of my own, and I actually posted it. David, of course, had no idea what I was up to. The ad read:

> We're a gay couple in New York that just celebrated our fourteenth anniversary and we've decided to extend our family. We're looking for someone close by and even have a separate apartment available if needed.

Nice, huh? Could it be just a little bit more . . . vague? Could my ad have lacked a little more personality? Sure, have our baby and move right in while you're doing it! Who the hell would respond to that? I wasn't even sure after reading it myself that it made any sense. But what should I have said? What could I have said? I scrambled to find a way to delete it, but couldn't.

Journal Entry, March 2002
I just posted an ad on a Web site dedicated to surrogacy. What have I done? I'm not sure it even makes sense. But, what's done is done. There's no taking it back.

> *What could I have said? "Two gay guys seek to procreate but can't for, well, obvious reasons. Need surrogate. Please be nice and seminormal. Please respond if your gene pool doesn't need a dose of chlorine."*

It was too late now. The ad had been posted. I had no idea what type of woman or how many would respond, if any at all, but our search was now officially in cyberspace for all and anyone to read. Now all I had to do was tell David. *Later,* I thought. *I'll do that later.*

But, while at the site, I couldn't resist checking out some of the ads that surrogates themselves had posted. The first thing that struck me was the lingo. It was like reading some strange foreign code. I had no idea what IP, IF, IM, FIM, GS, TS, RE, ED, DD, or DHD meant. Some I still don't. The only one missing was HCGG, or highly confused gay guy.

Anyway, fees started around $10,000. One experienced surrogate was asking $50,000. *That kid better be remarkable,* I thought. *It better be the next Picasso or Van Gogh.* "That must be some egg for fifty grand," one of my friends let slip. Additional fees were added for multiple babies, C-sections, lost wages, day care, health insurance, food, clothing, and on and on. Keep in mind that these were surrogates who had decided to go independent, meaning they weren't being represented by an agency. I couldn't believe it. Some said flat out that they wouldn't work with a gay couple, while others would be only a gestational surrogate. Some ads posted were from surrogates looking for a "good Christian couple"—nope, not us. Some had Web pages you could visit and e-mail addresses where you could reach them. It was like being in another world, and the longer I stayed, the more I started to realize that I was becoming more and more uncomfortable. Most of them had laid out their expectations loud and clear, and it seemed to all have to do with fees, reimbursements, and compensation—sometimes the list was more than ten items long.

Don't get me wrong; I knew why they had to be specific. I mean, if they were vague, like the lovely ad I had just posted, they would hear from every Tom, Dick, and Wacko, only having to explain everything over and over and over again.

I started thinking a little bit differently about the surrogate process. Seeing lists about money, timelines and payments, and attorneys and contracts bothered me, as it started to seem like more about making a business deal than bringing a baby into this world. I didn't like that feeling at all. What would I tell our child someday when they asked where they came from? Why was it important? I mean, if I were adopted, would I say, "Hey, Dad, Billie-Bob said his adoption cost fifty grand, but mine was only twenty-five, what gives?" The bottom line was that I was having serious second thoughts, but right before I left I came across this ad:

> 26-year-old, stable, mature, married, mother of two would like to help make your dreams of having a family a reality. I'm willing to be a TS or GS. I will work with straight or gay couples. Please visit my Web page for a list of my fees. All are negotiable.

I didn't waste any time before heading to her Web site to have a look-see. We also had about twenty-five responses from the ad that I posted, but none of them seemed as though they would pan out. "I won't work with a gay couple," one response said, "because I'm a devout Christian and don't believe in same-sex unions. But I did want to wish you luck and let you know of my services." Huh? Okay. Next! Others were pretty cut-and-dried. "I'm asking $25,000 as a flat fee, $5,000 for multiples, $5,000 for C-section, $500 a month living expenses, $1,500 for maternity clothes . . ." I couldn't even continue reading it, as she was already way out of our league. I did send her an e-mail though, suggesting that she should hook up with the high-priced agency on the West Coast.

I started to have a sinking feeling that this wasn't going to work after all. How were we going to be able to afford this? An adoption would have cost anywhere from $25,000 to $40,000, but a surrogacy arrangement looked like it could be a lot higher than that. However, thanks to my mother and father and a home equity line of credit, we were able to go forward.

Now, here's how I ended up going "first." One night while lying in bed again watching television, David turned to me during a commercial break and asked, "So, let's just say that we decide to have a child through surrogacy." I knew right then and there that I was in trouble—David rarely started a sentence with those words, so that meant he had something on his mind.

"It seems to only make sense," I said, cutting him off completely.

"Well," he continued, ignoring my interruption, "let's say we do. That leaves us with a really big question."

"Okay," I said.

"Well," he started to say, but stopped for another long pause—I was dying with anticipation. "With an adoption the child would be . . ." he hesitated again, "well, it wouldn't be our biological child."

"No," I said, "but, does that matter?"

"No, of course not," David replied. "But with surrogacy—if we do, in fact, decide to go through with something like this—which one of us would do it? I mean, go first? How would we ever decide that?"

I had no idea what to say or how to answer any of his questions. I was totally speechless—which was a first—on the outside, that is. On the inside I was screaming me, me, me, damn it, I'll go first! That's when I realized in my infinite wisdom that I knew what David was going to say. I had already taken it upon myself to figure it all out. Was I being selfish? You bet I was. I didn't like it. Nor did I want to admit it, but I had always just assumed that I would go first. Why? Maybe it was that I had done all the work. I made the phone calls, albeit not so well and ended up making a total fool of myself while doing so. Or, maybe it was that this whole thing was my idea. The fact is, I had many reasons.

I had also thought about David's schedule—which was bad, really, really bad. Because of that, he couldn't possibly dedicate very much time to making phone calls, researching, and answering questions. Plus, by the time we "got pregnant" and had the child, he would be a third-year resident. Our lives had already been turned upside down by his going to medical school at such a late stage in life. So, I think, at least *I think,* that's what I was thinking. See, I told you I had it all figured out. Or so I thought.

"Well," I said, struggling for words, "that's a good question. What do you think?"

I had learned from the best of the best, my friend Jennifer, that although it is highly annoying, the best thing to do when you are asked a question that you didn't have a clue how to answer was to simply answer by asking a question. Pretty neat, huh? For instance, if someone asks you what you think of their God-awful new hairstyle, you can either lie by saying that you can't believe he or she waited so long to get it cut like that, and risk being caught in your lie, or try the new trick that I had learned. You simply answer the question with a question of your own, such as, "I don't know. Do *you* like it?" It worked like a charm. Well, almost always. David would have no part of it.

"I think you've already made up your mind about who is going first," he said bluntly. Now I felt like a selfish ass. Not a partial ass— a complete, totally naked, bare, not to mention selfish, rear end. How could I have come to the conclusion that I wanted a biological child of my own without talking to David? We sat silently in bed for what seemed like hours before David broke the silence. "Just tell me why you should go first," he said.

"Well, I have the time," I started. "I can look into everything for us, even take some time off from work if I have to, and if everything goes okay I can then take three months off to stay home with the baby. Plus," I added while on a little bit of a roll, "the company I work for offers on-site day care, and it's cheap."

David sat silently, then asked if we would do it again. "I would hope so," I said. "It's something that we should plan on or at least ask about."

Then I was hit with an idea that I wasn't sure was flat-out stupid or the answer to our prayers.

"What about," I said, "if we don't have to decide which one of us goes first?" Judging by the look on his face, though, he didn't think it was such a swell idea.

"How the hell would we do that?" he asked.

"We could mix the sperm," I said. "That way we don't have to decide who goes first. It's kind of like, may the best sperm win." Yes, it was my sick attempt at humor and in case you're wondering, yes, it failed miserably.

"No," David said without any hesitation, "I don't think that works. If anything, it might result in our not getting pregnant at all. I think one of the reproductive specialists at the hospital said something about that once, where the sperm actually fight each other, or something."

"Sperm actually fight?" I asked with gross fascination.

"I don't really know," a starting-to-get-frustrated David replied. "Listen, you'll go first. I'll go next. It's obviously very important to you, Michael. It will give you something to sink your heart and soul into, and you'll be a wonderful father."

"Are you sure?" I asked.

"Yes," he said. "By the time we're ready to do this again, I'll be an attending physician somewhere, and I won't have these hours and this schedule."

That, as they say, was that. David promptly took the remote control from my hand and hit the unmute button so he could watch, and hear, the television.

> *Journal Entry, April 2002*
> *I got no sleep last night whatsoever. None. Zilch. Nada. Why?*
> *My mind was spinning again. This time I kept thinking about the*
> *baby-buying/baby-selling thing. Someone at work told me flat*
> *out that she thought what we were doing was the most disgust-*
> *ing thing she had ever heard of. I knew there would be some peo-*
> *ple that would have a problem with what we were doing, but to*
> *say that it was the most disgusting thing she had ever heard*
> *wasn't what I had expected. I can think of many, many, more*
> *things that I find more disgusting—her 1980s hairstyle for one.*
> *Are David and I really going to buy a baby? Was a woman really*
> *going to sell us a baby? It sounds dreadful, but I'm not sure what*
> *the hell to do.*

I knew that I needed to make yet another phone call to our agency after having tossed and turned all night. The day before I had made the mistake of telling someone at work—someone who I thought was a friend—all about what David and I were doing. I wanted to share the news, the excitement of it all, and hopefully gain some much-needed support. Boy, was I ever in for a shock.

"That's the most disgusting thing I've ever heard of people doing," my stunned co-worker said with a huge scowl on her face. "How could a woman possibly set out to have a child, only to know that she was going to hand it over to someone at the end? And, she's getting paid for doing it? That's just disgusting."

At first, I was speechless. My mind was racing. The shock of someone being so honest about their feelings just wasn't settling in. "She's always wanted to do this," I said with a puzzled look on my face. "No one is making her do it and believe me, for what she's being reimbursed she's either nuts or doesn't need the money, because it's honestly not that much."

"It's disgusting," she said flatly. "She's either incredibly desperate or flat-out crazy. Either way, she's doing nothing more than selling her very own child and you guys are doing nothing more than buying it from her."

"I just wish you could tell me how you really feel about all of this," I said, trying to calm her down.

"You don't even know who this person is," she continued unabashedly. "You met her online, for God's sake. How do you meet someone on the Internet one week and decide to have a child with her the next?"

Good question, I thought to myself.

"It's not as if we met her yesterday," I said, trying to explain. "We met several weeks ago. Plus, we're working with an agency." I wasn't about to back down, and I didn't. "It's easy for you to judge," I said flatly. "You are a fertile woman, or so you think, and can have a child with or without a man being directly involved. It's different for us. It's just different. You could call sperm-banks-are-us tomorrow and have a child next year."

"No," she fired back, "I wouldn't have a child without a husband. A child needs a mother and a father. So, no, thank you, I wouldn't have a child for that very same reason, and I cannot believe that there are actually agencies out there that do this kind of thing."

I'm sure our co-workers down the hall from us were either glued to their office walls by now or had run away. I was also wondering if this co-worker now regretted asking how my weekend was. Keep in mind that I had heard this song and dance before. All that was missing was a mixed drink, an elf suit, and a large bank account.

"So, let me get this straight," I said in a rare moment of clarity. "Your father left your family when you were four years old, correct?"

"Yes," she said, "thanks for bringing that up and reminding me of it."

Ouch.

"So," I continued before forgetting my point, "if your logic holds true about a child needing a mother and a father, then someone should have come to your house and taken you away, right?"

"That's absurd," she said, getting angrier by the moment.

"But," I said, "you weren't raised by a mother and a father because your mother kicked your father to the curb. So, you were raised in a single-parent household. You no longer had a mother and a father at home. Following your logic, or lack thereof, shouldn't Child Protective Services have come to your door to whisk you away from the evil single-parent household?"

"It's different," she said. "My mother didn't set out to be a single parent."

"I'm not a single parent either," I said. "Or did you forget that David and I have been together for almost fifteen years?"

"It's not the same," she said adamantly. "What do two gay men know about caring for a baby, let alone raising a child?"

"So because I'm a man I don't know anything about caring for a child?" I asked in disbelief.

"A child needs a mother, a female influence in the house. So how are you going to handle that one?" she shot back.

"I don't have all the answers," I said. "I really don't. But I do know that our child will have women in his or her life. My mother and sister, for example, just to name two."

"Two men do not know anything about raising a child. It's wrong. You'll see. It's wrong. Let alone how you're bringing the child into this world."

"The point is," I said, finally remembering my point to begin with, "people don't always have mothers and fathers who lived together and raised them, and yet they grow up just fine."

We were clearly getting nowhere. But she wasn't backing down and neither was I.

"I don't think God intended for two men to raise a baby together," she said, pulling the religion card out of her pocket as a last resort. "As a matter of fact, it's a sin, and if it isn't, it should be."

"People who live in glass cathedrals shouldn't be tossing stones at my glass shack," I fired back, now angry. "The next time your boyfriend blows into town, and the two of you are knockin' boots out of wedlock, I'll put in a friendly phone call to a local priest and he can come over and throw some holy water on the two of you to cleanse your sins!"

She didn't answer, just glared at me. So far this day had gone horribly, and it was Monday to boot.

"That woman is selling her own child to you for a price," she finally managed to say, while pointing her finger at me, "and it deeply disgusts me."

"Well," I said, "our alternative is to adopt, and money changes hands with that, too. Does that make adoptions disgusting too? We've thought about it a lot and think that it's imperative for our child to know that he or she does in fact have a biological mother. I also want our child to know his or her birth mother."

"That's just going to confuse the hell out of the child, don't you think?" she asked.

"Actually," I said, "no. It's one more person who loves the child and wants only the best that life can bring. So, it's one more person that he or she can go to for love and support."

She wasn't buying any of what I had to say. We went back and forth like that for nearly an hour.

"What about this child? How are you ever going to explain this?" she asked.

"That's a good question," I said, starting to calm down. "Look. I think what a child needs more than anything in life is to be loved unconditionally. That's how I would explain it. We loved you so much that we were willing to go to great lengths to bring you into this world."

It still wasn't working, and I finally realized that, although we weren't angry with each other anymore, it was time that I got up and left. Needless to say, our friendship and working relationship would never recover.

Even though I was rattled by our conversation, I actually walked away feeling very good about myself. She hadn't asked me one single question that I hadn't already thought of. It actually helped me, a little bit, to come to terms with some of the issues that I was still having, as I could answer all of her questions truthfully and without hesitation. What kept going through my mind afterward was the baby-selling and baby-buying comment. Is that what David and I were really going to do? Were we really going to buy a baby from a woman who was selling one?

Once our agency finally answered the telephone, I asked the director where this term of baby-buying and baby-selling had come from. "That term actually comes from the courts," the director said, "where they are in the middle of a contract dispute and some contracts stipulate that a surrogate is paid one lump sum only after the child is delivered and the parents take custody. Generally they are reimbursed on a monthly basis, with final payment, or reimbursement, made after the child is born." I was shocked, to say the least. First, the terminology, and how it would have to be interchanged all the time.

"Was it reimbursement or compensation?" I asked.

"It depends on where the people drew up the contract. Some courts, or judges," he went on to explain, "feel that it's flat-out buying a baby and selling a baby if there is a lump sum payment at the end of the pregnancy, since receiving the money depends on the surrogate surrendering the child. No child means no money. So that's where that term came from."

I could completely understand that concept. I mean, it wouldn't seem fair to withhold a large sum of money until the very end and use it as kind of a carrot at the end of a stick. Actually, it seemed cruel.

"You'll also find that surrogates themselves have issues with it," the director added.

"Issues with surrogacy?" I asked.

"Issues with being a gestational surrogate versus a traditional surrogate, yes. By and large, most surrogates are gestational. Many surrogates can't fathom having a biological connection to the child, so you will see some pretty heated arguments arising on some of the surrogacy message boards, especially regarding traditional surrogacy."

At the time I couldn't believe that surrogates actually discriminated against one another, but I would go on to witness it myself several times.

While we were talking, the word "contract" kept coming up, but I had never heard anything about it before, and we certainly didn't have one sitting in front of us. "Will we have this contract drawn up, too?" I finally asked.

"Yes," I was told, "you will, once you find a surrogate, that is." *Good point,* I thought.

The director went on to explain that we wouldn't be able to have a contract drawn up and signed in New York, where we live, as it's not legal to do so. As far as I understood it, what we were doing wasn't illegal, in that the cops would knock down our door and take us away to the local slammer. However, if we did have a dispute over something in the contract, New York State wasn't about to hear the case in their court system. Not a good thing. Once we found a surrogate, the contract would be drawn up and signed in the state where the child would be born.

"They generally run anywhere from ten to twenty pages long," the director explained about the contract, "but I don't see yours running longer than five or six. It's pretty cut-and-dried."

Journal Entry, April 2002
What are we doing? What am I doing? This is all just happening
way too fast. We've signed a contract with an agency and writ-
ten them a check for thousands of dollars. I've put an ad on the
Internet looking for a surrogate mother and went to her Web
site. I'm fighting with friends at work. My family thinks I'm
crazy. I am crazy! This is crazy! Are we really doing this? Are we
doing the right thing? Wouldn't it be a hell of a lot easier to just
adopt? We could do an open adoption where the kid would know
his or her birth mother and be done with it. A least that way we
aren't fighting with family, friends, and co-workers about any-
thing. No. No. No. What about me? I would love nothing more
than a child of my own. Why do I have to defend that? Do Bob
and Sue Blue have to defend their desire to be parents to some-
one at work? I don't think so. They don't have two teeth in their
heads between the two of them, but no one would ever question
their desire, let alone right, to have a child. Would they? What
about this child? It is really being fair? Can the child really have
a normal, healthy, happy life if people are telling me now that
what we're doing is disgusting? One thing for damn sure is that
we'd better figure this all out before we even think about going
any further.

After weeks of phone calls, e-mails, searching the Internet, writing
checks, asking questions, and being pummeled with internal questions, I started having serious doubts about what we were doing. I
didn't doubt my desire to be a parent, because I had always dreamed
of having a family. I just never thought it would happen. What I did
start to doubt, again, was whether my wanting to be a parent was in
the best interest of my child. I kept replaying the conversation that I
had with my co-worker and how often she used the term "disgusting"
to describe how she felt about what we were doing. I could vividly remember her pointing her finger right at me and telling me that we
were "buying a baby." If people thought that way, then how could our
child ever have a normal life? In the end, it all boiled down to one simple question: Why surrogacy and why not adoption?

In short, the answer was simple. I wanted a child of my own. I
wanted a biological child. Why wouldn't I? It sounds simple, but it
took me many years to come to that conclusion. I thought of all the
children that were waiting for, and needed, loving homes. I thought of

all the special needs children that were waiting for homes, and how wonderful it would be to raise them with love and self-confidence. However, I also wondered why everyone, fertile or infertile, didn't adopt a child rather than have a child of their own. All I knew was that I had always dreamed of having a child of my very own. It felt strange. It felt selfish. It felt wrong. It felt wonderful. It's a feeling that I can't adequately describe.

I also thought about how amazing it would be for our child to actually know his or her birth mother. Obviously, being two men, our child would turn to us at some point and wonder how two men could have a baby; but more than that, wouldn't having the birth mother in the child's life mean that he or she would have one more person that loved, cherished, and wanted nothing but the best in life for him or her?

"I think so," David said one night while we talked about our fears. "I think we have to be honest with our child, about how he or she came to be, right from the very start. Otherwise, we're starting out with a lie."

"What about our child being teased and tormented by other kids?" I asked.

"There's no doubt that kids can be cruel," David looked at me and said. "If you're short, fat, thin, wear glasses, are rich or poor, it doesn't matter. If you're different, you get picked on." He then asked me what I thought.

"I think the difference is that we know our child is going to face ridicule, and maybe we can prepare for it. I mean, my parents didn't know that I was gay until I was in my early twenties. Had they known earlier—had I told them earlier—maybe they could have helped me cope with it better."

The truth is, we'll probably never know all the answers. How does anyone know?

In any event, the ball was definitely rolling—sometimes it would roll on its own and other times I had to give it a gentle push or flat-out shove to help it along a little bit. One thing was for certain: we had no idea what we were getting ourselves into. We just had to either stay behind the ball or get completely run over by it.

–2–

Getting Started

Journal Entry, April 2002
I went to the Web site of a potential surrogate yesterday. Her
name is Michelle. She seems perfect. She's twenty-six years old,
married, and has two kids of her own. Apparently, her husband,
James, is okay with her being a surrogate, even for a gay couple.
Her fees are in line with what we can afford, so I'm keeping my
fingers crossed. I'm excited, but desperately trying not to get my
hopes up. I still have to tell David about that ad, don't I? It prob-
ably wouldn't hurt to tell him about Michelle either, for that
matter. Don't you think?

I sent Michelle a "Hi, how do you do?" e-mail after going to her Web site, and it didn't take long for her to write back. What surprised me the most, while looking over her Web page, was how much time and thought she had given to being a traditional surrogate mother. She had included pictures of her and her family, a get-to-know-me type page complete with a summary of why she wanted to be a surrogate, and a page that listed fees and such. Within a day she wrote back. I couldn't believe that she had responded so quickly, nor could I believe how excited I was. She thanked me for visiting her site and then asked if we were working with an agency. After I told her which one, she said, much to my surprise, that she was, in fact, listed with the very same one that we were. If that were the case, then where was her profile? "I might still be listed as a gestational surrogate," she explained. "I wanted to be listed under both traditional and gestational, so I'll call them and try to get to the bottom of it." I also sent out an e-mail to the agency, asking why she wasn't listed.

In the meantime, we kept writing getting-to-know-you e-mails back and forth nearly every single day. It was exciting, yet nerve-wracking. Things were just moving so quickly. Within days her name and profile appeared on the agency's Web site. Imagine that.

"You did what?" a surprised David asked, after I had told him that I had not only placed an ad on a surrogacy Web site, but that I had been talking to a potential surrogate for several days.

"Well," I tried my best to explain, "everything just kind of happened so fast. I found the Web site and like I said, I e-mailed Michelle, and she e-mailed me back."

"Does she work with our agency? Is she signed up with the same one?" David asked as his mind raced with questions. "We don't even know her!"

"We're working all of that stuff out," I said, trying to reassure him that I hadn't gone and signed a contract, let alone started trying to get pregnant yet.

"Have you talked to her yet?" he asked with a huge smile.

"Only through e-mails; not on the telephone or anything," I said. "I wouldn't do that without you."

"Well, that's good! I can't believe it though!" he said emphatically.

Every morning when I woke up I immediately signed on to check e-mails. All the while, I kept asking myself if it was realistic to think that we could get to know someone well enough to carry our child so fast. Even though our e-mails were more fact filled than anything, covering subjects such as where we worked and what we liked and didn't like, it felt as though we were laying the foundation for a strong friendship. Sometimes, it even felt as though we had known each other for a lot longer than several weeks.

Among other things, she wanted to know what we were looking for in a traditional surrogate and why we chose surrogacy and not adoption. I did most, if not all, of the writing back and forth, as David isn't as compelled as I am to spend hours sitting at the computer. To keep him in the loop, I would just print out the e-mails for him to read later. He was starting to get just as excited as I was.

One thing was for sure, her questions were certainly giving us a lot to think about. "I'm glad that I'm able to ask you questions to make you think," Michelle wrote. "Honestly, though, that's kind of my job. I have to make sure you all are going to be good parents. You just have to make sure you can get along with me, and that I will take care of my body while taking care of your little angel!"

lated risk, but a risk nonetheless. I kept telling myself and others that
if Michelle, or any other surrogate that we ended up working with,
did end up not wanting to give the child up, that I would be the biolog‑
ical father, and thereby have some legal rights. If we were to face the
same dilemma in an adoption scenario, I wasn't sure what rights
either of us would have.

I kept writing e-mails and asking questions, as did Michelle. "I
work a full-time job and I'm the mother of two kids," she wrote. "I'm
done with my family. I have a boy and a girl and that's exactly what
we wanted to have. So, we're done. So done that it's permanent. My
husband and I can't have any more children, ever." I didn't press her
on the subject, but I assumed that she meant her hubby had gone and
had a snip done. Michelle later confirmed that he had in fact had a
vasectomy.

"So, how do we know for sure that you won't change your mind?"
I asked her in one e-mail.

"I'm not really sure that there is anything I can say to reassure a
couple that I won't change my mind," she replied. "All I can say is
that my family is complete. We've made our decision to quit having
children."

"The only thing that I'm really concerned about," she confided, "is
that I know my current weight may be a concern."

I asked her what she meant.

"I don't even look my weight," she said. "I just gained seventy
pounds with my son and after his birth I lost very little of the weight."

I wasn't sure what to say. David, being a resident in obstetrics, had
come home from work once in a while saying that an overweight pa‑
tient had come in with complications. "It's mostly blood pressure
concerns," I asked, "right?"

"I was just as heavy as I am now when I had my daughter,"
Michelle wrote, "and I had zero complications with that pregnancy. I
don't want it to be an issue. I don't want to be judged. That's all I ask.

If you do judge me, judge me for who, and what, I am, not how much I weigh."

With that said, I talked to David about it. He was mildly concerned, but not freaked out to the point of saying no way in hell should we keep talking with her. The fact of the matter was she had had two successful pregnancies, had lived to tell about them, and wanted to do it again.

I began to realize just how many details we would need to discuss, and at times I felt overwhelmed. However, we pressed on. Next up was health insurance. "I'm under both my insurance through work and my husband's insurance," Michelle wrote, "but he is planning on taking me off of it. My insurance through work is so much better, but it doesn't cover surrogacy. His covers the pregnancy but not fertility treatments, which we don't need to worry about. So, I'm not sure what you want to do about that."

I wasn't sure either. David and I talked about it and figured that since she was covered under two different insurance policies, at least for another six months, we didn't have anything to worry about. Believe me, it was a nonchalant attitude that we would come to deeply regret.

We decided to set up a time for the three of us to speak on the telephone. Of course, I spent the entire week obsessing over it. We called Michelle at a designated time on a Saturday afternoon. At first it was very awkward, but it ended up being a lot easier than I had expected. We talked about everything and anything, from our desire to have children to what kind of couple she was hoping to help.

"Commitment," she said, "is probably the most important thing to me. I'm looking to help a couple that has been together at least four years, who are committed to each other and to having a child. I don't want someone who is desperate," I remember her saying. "I don't want someone who sees this as a last resort, but someone who sees it as as a wonderful experience. I also want someone who is as eager as I am to bring a baby into this world."

She was intelligent, hardworking, down-to-earth, personable, and seemed to be doing this for all the right reasons. We were hooked.

"So," she asked, "why do you guys want to have a child?"

"Well," David started, "we've been together for fourteen years now and it's just come to a time in our relationship where we are ready to have a child. We're settled. We're so settled, we're dead. Having a child would take us to the next level in our relationship."

Michelle laughed. That's what was especially nice about talking to her—we didn't have to explain anything. She knew we were gay, she knew that we lived across the country from her, and she knew we wanted to have kids and why. We didn't have to justify, or explain, or worry that she would have an issue with our being gay.

"I've just always wanted to be a father," I said. "It's an instinct that I've had for a very long time now. It seems to be the right time, and place, for us to do it right now."

We were also impressed by the fact that becoming a traditional surrogate wasn't something she took lightly.

"It took me four years to get to the point," she said, "mentally and financially, to be able to pursue this. I've given it a lot of thought, and it wasn't a decision that I took lightly."

I asked her how her husband felt about all of this and what she would tell her kids if and when she started showing signs of being pregnant.

"Well," she said, "I honestly don't know what I'm going to tell the kids. They are five and six, so they are old enough to ask embarrassing questions. But I don't know what I will tell them. It would definitely be something that we would have to talk about, though, as they would be siblings. But right now, at this very moment, I honestly don't know what I would tell them."

We liked that answer—she didn't have all the answers, and didn't have to. How could someone have the answers to every single question?

"As far as my husband goes," she went on, "well, it took him a while to get used to it all."

"So, why do you want to work with a gay couple?" I asked.

"A very good friend of mine is gay, and I've talked to him about having kids," she explained cheerfully. "I'm not sure, but I think he tried to adopt and it didn't work out. I don't think that it's fair that a gay couple, like you, can't have children of your own. So that's why I'm doing it."

"From what I've seen," I said, "and from some of the e-mails we've gotten, it seems that most surrogates won't work with a gay couple."

After a long pause she said, "I mean, don't get me wrong. I thought about working with a straight couple, once or twice, but then I heard a lot of stories from other surrogates about how the intended mother, if she was the infertile one, would sometimes end up having a lot of issues with the surrogate."

I asked her what she meant.

"Well," she tried to explain, "if the wife is infertile she has to sit back and watch as her husband gets another woman pregnant. Not only that, but then she has to watch that same woman carry and deliver her husband's child. That would be really hard, you know?"

"Wow," I said, "yeah, that sounds pretty complicated."

David then asked her how hard she thought it would be when people who knew her, knew that she and her husband were done having kids, saw that she was pregnant. "How will you explain it?" he asked.

There was a long pause, and then with a giggle Michelle said, "Well, if they ask when James is standing there he'll probably chime right in and tell them off. He would tell them flat out that it's none of their business and probably walk away." She laughed again and said, "If it's me and I'm alone I don't know what I would say. Well, I would probably say that it's either none of their business or that I'm a surrogate mother."

I remember David and me just looking at each other and thinking, *Wow, that would take a lot of guts, wouldn't it?* But neither of us had any doubts that Michelle or James wouldn't do as she said.

"I'm going to be out in public, you know," Michelle went on, "so I'll have to get used to people asking. I'll just have to wait and see what kind of a mood I'm in that day!"

We talked a little more and then it was time to ask whether she wanted to work with us as much as we wanted to work with her. "So," I asked hesitantly, "what do you think, Michelle? Do you think you'd like to work with us?"

There was a pause. Then she said, "I have no doubt. No doubt whatsoever."

All three of us laughed, and then Michelle started to cry. "It will be wonderful," she said. "I promise it will be wonderful."

We then talked about going to meet her and her family in Nevada. However, before making any definite plans or agreeing to actually do it, I still had something on my mind—the part where she had said that it took awhile for her husband to agree to her doing a traditional surrogacy. I kept wondering how a straight guy could be happy about seeing his wife walking around pregnant with someone else's baby—

let alone the baby for two gay guys. "What, if anything," I asked, "did you have to say to James before he changed his mind?"

"He knew that I wanted to be a surrogate," she explained. "I started talking about it right after my son was born. At first, I was going to be a gestational surrogate, and he was fine with it after a while. Then when I told him that I wanted to be a traditional surrogate, he didn't exactly freak, but he was really surprised. He didn't," she added, "know exactly what to say to that."

What could he say other than no way in hell? I thought.

"Is this the kind of thing," I asked, thinking to myself that she's only twenty-six years old, "that you would do with or without your husband's support?"

"No," she answered without hesitation, "I wouldn't do this if James wasn't behind it one hundred percent."

"Well," I said, "he must be one hell of a confident and secure straight guy, or he's nuts, or he's being forced into doing something that he doesn't want to do, as it's either this or divorce, right?"

"No," Michelle said quickly, "he's not being forced into doing anything. James would never do what he didn't want to do and he wouldn't let someone, anyone, including me, tell him what to do or stop him from doing something that he wanted to do."

We later found out just how true Michelle's assessment of James really was. I still wasn't completely fearless, even after Michelle tried to explain, but I knew she had said all that she could.

"Is it going to bother you that we live so far away?" David jumped in and asked.

"I'd expect you to be at the major appointments," she said bluntly, "but I don't expect you to be at all of them. As a matter of fact, I think it would drive me crazy to have you there all the time."

"Why?" I asked.

"Because you're men," she said with a laugh. "You're gay, but you're still men! I've been through this before, you know, twice now, and it can get pretty rough toward the end, but I'll be fine."

"It's all a matter of trust, I guess?" I blurted out.

"Definitely," she said. "I have to trust that you're doing this for all the right reasons, and you have to do the same."

The last subject that I remember coming up was how much contact she expected to have with us after the child was born. Would she want to meet him or her and eventually know him or her after the child was born? It was a major issue for many couples, from what I had read at different surrogate Web sites.

"I would prefer to remain friends with you guys after the baby is born," she explained, "but it's entirely up to you. I would be happy with at least an e-mail once in a while and a picture of the family once a year. In all honesty, though," she continued, "I would leave that up to you. No one really knows right now what they will be comfortable with, so it's hard to say."

"Would you want to meet him or her some day?" I asked.

"I think that would be a great thing. I would just be curious, you know? Curious how the family and child matured. What he or she looked like and that kind of thing," Michelle said without hesitation. So, it didn't seem as though she would stalk us mercilessly.

"It's really important to us," I said, "that this child knows you, and that you are a part of his or her life. The child wouldn't be here if it weren't for you, so it's very important for us to be open about this from the moment the child can even begin to understand how he or she came to be."

"That's great!" Michelle said enthusiastically. "Like I said before, it's really up to you guys. I don't want to tell any intended parents how it has to be. It's really up to you. But I'd love it. It doesn't sound like you guys want, or need, a co-parent or anything, and I'm not looking for that either."

Before hanging up we made a promise to each other that we would be completely honest throughout our journey. It's something that would come back to challenge me.

"Tell us everything that you are thinking and feeling, Michelle, even if it's the worst," I said. "That way, we won't break your heart and you won't break ours."

"It's going to be great," Michelle said through tears. "It's going to be a wonderful experience. You're going to be daddies!"

We hung up the phone and the first words out of David's mouth were, "She's perfect. She's just perfect."

My parents were here visiting for the weekend, and I remember going outside and telling my mom that I felt like I was in a complete fog. It seemed so unreal to me that we had just gotten off the phone with someone 3,000 miles away whom we've never met, but who was going to help us have a child. I was also worried about my parents' reaction. It's not every day that your gay son comes to sit down next to you to tell you all about the surrogate who's going to have his child, you know? "It's funny isn't it," Mom said. "We can dream about something happening, and want it to happen so much. But when the dream starts coming true, little by little, inch by inch, there's this feeling that this can't be happening. Well, it is happening, Mike, and you and David deserve it to happen."

"As long as she knows what she's doing and you guys both know what you're getting into," my dad chimed in, "everything will work out. You have to trust your instincts. If your instincts are telling you that it's going to work out and everything will be fine, then you should trust them. Listen to yourself and don't doubt what you're thinking. You'll be fine."

Our next hurdle was having a contract drawn up that satisfied everyone. We had paid our agency a separate fee for drawing it all up, and they would also act as the middleman by handling all the negotiations. At least, that was the plan. We would then send it off to our attorney and to Michelle's attorney, for whom we would pay. That's how the process was supposed to work, anyway. Our agency was supposed to contact each of us separately to go over everything in detail, then draw up the contract and send it out to us for our review. However, that's not quite how it ended up working. Days of waiting for the contract turned into weeks, and the weeks turned into almost two months. Michelle and I started to become very irritated, as we were anxious to get started. Believe it or not, after several e-mails back and forth and a phone call, we agreed that we would forge ahead on our own. Yes, on our own.

I wrote a final e-mail to the agency, letting them know that we were about to go ahead with the contract without them. A week later a response arrived warning me not to talk about anything even remotely having to do with money, finances, or compensation. "You're risking getting into some very delicate subjects here," the agency said in the e-mail, "and we would strongly advise that you avoid the subject of money altogether."

"We can work things out," I wrote to Michelle. "The only thing we aren't supposed to talk about is the money aspect."

"I think we can, too," she wrote back. "If we don't, we'll probably be waiting a very, very, long time."

I was so relieved, because now that we had found Michelle, the last thing that I wanted to have happen was for her to grow increasingly disgusted to the point where she would consider working with another couple. Besides, it was clear from our conversations and e-mails that Michelle knew a great deal about the subject of contracts, as she seemed to have a very good support system of fellow surrogates.

Everything went very well at first. Michelle had listed most of the fees and money matters on her Web site, so I didn't think there would be any shockers there.

I was surprised to find out, however, that we would pay for everything related to the pregnancy. When I say everything, I mean everything, including Michelle's fee for carrying the child—or living expenses, as they were later referred to in our contract—plus all medical bills that aren't picked up by her insurance. An additional fee applied for multiple babies, and another if a C-section had to be performed. She would also receive a maternity clothes allowance, bed rest, child care, housekeeping, lost wages, all legal expenses, and all travel and accommodations. Plus, additional fees were included to cover vitamins, pregnancy tests, ovulation predictor kits, and so on.

It was all a lot to absorb. "I wouldn't do it for that little money," our friend Sally said to us later that night at dinner, "but if you offered me fifty grand I might carry a horse to full term!"

In the meantime, I would feed everything back via e-mails to our agency so that they could be added into the contract. Finally, after a couple of weeks, David and I received the tentative contract. I was shocked to see that it was fifteen pages long and filled with things that we had never even begun to think about. It was also wrong. As I was scanning down the pages, I came across the subject of who would take custody of "said child" should David and I meet our untimely demise. A name appeared in the blank. The only problem was that it wasn't someone we knew! I recognized the person's last name immediately becasue it was the same last name as the director of the agency. During one of our original conversations we found out that the director was a parent via surrogacy. It was obvious that what we had just paid $2,500 for was a copy of a contract, not an original. I was furious and reached for the phone, only to hear a busy signal on the other end, or the lovely and talented answering machine. I left a message, basically stating, "The contract came and obviously it's the one you used for your own surrogacy as you forgot to take out one of your family member's names. Fix it and send us another contract immediately." It was a red flag of many things to come, but unfortunately I was too fixated on working out the contract to worry about anything else.

David and I looked that contract over with a fine-tooth comb and spotted a few things that we had questions about, including money. Another e-mail and phone call to the agency. Again, no response. So, once again, Michelle and I forged ahead on our own. Against the agency's advice, we ended up discussing everything from fees to re-imbursements. It ended up being a big mistake, as I simply couldn't handle it.

Journal Entry, April 2002
I couldn't sleep again last night. I actually woke up in the middle of the night and was furious. Our agency has done nothing, ab-solutely nothing. Not worth their fee, that's for sure. It takes for-ever to get in touch with them. Plus, my teeth feel funny this morning too! So I looked in the mirror and noticed that my front teeth were chipped a little bit. What the hell is that? I think I'm grinding my teeth again.

Reading over the contract proved to be extremely difficult and stressful for us because it was filled with numbers, figures, legal jar-gon, and many, many things that we didn't expect to see. After look-ing it over and talking about it, we realized that there really wasn't much to change on our end, so we waited to hear back from Michelle. Everything seemed to be pretty cut-and-dried. I certainly didn't ex-pect to react the way that I did once Michelle had a chance to e-mail her questions and changes. As a matter of fact, I honestly thought for the first time that things were going to fall through. Getting through the contract phase, as it's called, was going to be more difficult than I had ever imagined. Looking back, I see we should have left it up to the agency. It just might have taken a year or two.

For all of us, talking about money and a baby in the same breath was excruciating. Negotiating fees and money seemed unconsciona-ble. Michelle's requests were more than reasonable. It was talking about it all that was so difficult. One stumbling block was an insemi-nation fee, whereby a fee was paid every time we did a round of inseminations. We had talked briefly about doing in-home, or do-it-yourself, inseminations, so I wondered why we were going to pay ev-ery time we did it. Plus, Michelle was going to track her own cycle with a program she had found online that helped her determine when she was ovulating. I sent her an e-mail about it and she agreed to drop the fee without really giving me an answer or explanation.

Then, the subject of paying for her and her husband's lost wages from work was broached. "If I need a day off from work," Michelle explained, "it really wouldn't be fair if I had to take a sick day or a vacation day. The same goes for my husband. Why should he have to take a vacation day to help me with anything related to my being pregnant when it's not his child?"

They were questions that I wasn't the least bit ready to answer. "Well," I said, fumbling for a response, "I assume that you guys talked about this a lot before you decided to get into it, right? And, to me, that means that you're going to have to do some things every now and then that are related to the pregnancy, like take a day off from work or use a sick day. That's what the compensation is for, right? It's a fifty-fifty deal, isn't it?"

Michelle clearly didn't know what I was trying to say. I wasn't sure if I knew either.

"I guess I don't understand why you're being compensated, then." I asked much to my own surprise. "What exactly is the compensation for?"

"It's for pain and suffering," she replied. "It's all related to carrying your child, not mine."

"I think I'm just having trouble understanding it all," I wrote in an e-mail. "It's all new to me and I have a lot to think about and figure out, I guess. It seems as though some of these fees should come out of the compensation. Paying for vacation days, sick days, and personal time for both you and James is going to add up very quickly. It could get really expensive and it's not something that we had planned for."

"As a rule," Michelle explained in her reply, "surrogates don't pay for anything related to the pregnancy. You guys pay for everything; as you should. Not one dime comes out of the surrogate's pocket," she stated firmly but still rather cheerfully, as though not to send us packing. "I have to look out for my own family here, and I can't take money out of their pockets to have your child."

I was surprised, to say the least. It didn't sound as though there was any room for negotiation, and that wasn't making me feel terribly comfortable. We were all getting into some really unknown territory and it was all becoming very, very complicated. I don't know why, but I hadn't expected it to.

Slowly but surely we started to work things out. It might sound as if our e-mails were filled with we'll do this, we won't do that, and constant talk about money, but that honestly wasn't the case. It was actually one of the most exciting times in our journey. We had found someone who was willing to carry a child for us. That was, and still is, such an amazing feeling. It was all just entirely new territory for me, and I obviously, with my teeth grinding, wasn't dealing with the stress of it very well. After a week or two, things got to a point where I thought we were all happy with the contract. We hadn't sought out legal advice and neither had Michelle. Also, to keep things less personal, we handled the majority of it through e-mails.

"So, how are you guys making out?" David asked one night.

"We weren't, at first," I said, "but now we seem to be working things out. I think we're done. I really think we're done."

Then Michelle sent another e-mail. "I don't see anything in the contract about mileage," she wrote, "so we need to talk about that, I think."

I wasn't sure what she meant by mileage.

"Gas mileage," she wrote, "for my driving back and forth to the doctor's appointments."

I hadn't seen that one coming and nearly fell out of my chair. The stress of everything was quickly getting the best of me. I was in a state of disbelief.

"How far is the doctor's office?" I asked.

"It's about a thirty-mile drive one way. The office is actually across the state line in California, but I'll be driving there from work, not from home, so it's a little bit farther for me to go," she replied.

I didn't know where to even begin. The question of paying for gas mileage just seemed to come right out of left field. I couldn't believe that after agreeing to pay all the other fees, reimbursements, and expenses we were now being asked to pay for gas mileage. I asked David what he thought.

"Why?" he asked. "Why would we pay for gas mileage?"

Good question, I thought. *I have to ask Michelle.*

"I don't think it's fair," she explained, "that I should have to take money out of my pocket to put gas in my car to go to a doctor's appointment for your baby."

I didn't have an answer, just a raised eyebrow. I kept wondering how much it could possibly cost to put gas in her car. The more I thought about it, the angrier I got. I also started feeling that we were being taken advantage of, as if money wasn't an object for us.

"Okay," I wrote, "since it looks like you're not going to budge on this one, how much are you expecting?"

"I think the going rate is about thirty-six or thirty-eight cents a mile," she wrote, "and I think that's more than fair."

All I kept asking myself was: If someone is doing something out of the goodness of her heart or doing something because she truly wanted to help you, would she really ask you to pay for their gas mileage?

> *Journal Entry, April 2002*
> *I'm still not sleeping at all. Going over this contract with Michelle has proved to be a huge mistake for me. I can't handle it. Between work and David being gone a lot this month I'm completely stressed. This gas mileage thing is going to drive me crazy. Why isn't it part of the compensation? I mean, what the hell is she driving around in out there, a tank? So, get this, I've noticed that people have been staring at me lately. No, it's not paranoia. The past few weeks' people have been staring at me when I'm talking to them. First they stare at me, then they look away with this weird look on their face. What the hell is up with that? Then, yesterday, believe it or not, someone called me "Twitch." Come to find out, people are staring at me because I've developed some kind of nervous twitch in my lower eyelid. So, now I am officially a freak. I can't sleep. I grind my teeth at night and now I twitch. I told David about it last night. He said he wished something else on me twitched. He's a real riot.*

I was obviously angry, but what was I angry about? One of the issues bothering me was that I thought Michelle and I had become friends. I was also starting to feel really bad about myself. Am I a monster? Some creep that doesn't appreciate what Michelle is doing for us? How petty can I be? Am I the kind of person that expects her to take money out of her own pocket for me or for my child? This wasn't what friends did. Friends didn't argue over gas mileage. Then I started questioning whether or not we could truly be friends, given the circumstances. You know? I mean, usually, you meet friends at work, or through other friends. Either you like each other and hit it off, or you don't. Michelle and I were trying to develop a friendship with an agenda, so to speak, because we both came into the friendship wanting to get something out of it. Could we really be friends and both have such ulterior motives?

It was that question that sent me into having a complete and total meltdown. I didn't e-mail Michelle for days, and if the subject came up I was on the verge of tears. I was also quickly becoming a complete mess. It didn't help matters that our agency was right about our not getting into all of these subjects. The nights of not getting any sleep and the stress of it all were starting to show. I had noticed that people were staring at me lately. I couldn't for the life of me figure out why. I would run into the bathroom to make sure I didn't have something stuck to my teeth—I had been grinding them lately, so God only knows what could have been caught on the jagged little edges I had created in my sleep. Then, one day, a co-worker of mine passed me in the hallway and said, "Hey, good morning, Twitch!" Twitch? What the hell kind of nickname is that? I went after her and asked her what she meant.

"Oh, well," she stumbled, "your eye. It's . . . well . . . it moves."

"Of course my eye moves!" I said. I'm sure I looked completely crazed.

"Well . . ." she stumbled again while slowly starting to back away, "it . . . well . . . it kind of twitches . . . a little bit."

"My eye twitches? What the hell does that mean?" I asked.

Come to find out my lower eyelid twitched. So, I was now a complete and total freak. I wasn't eating, or sleeping, would soon have little nubs for teeth from grinding them in my sleep, and now I was twitching. David offered little or no solace.

"I've never seen it before," he said while staring at me, but trying not to stare at me, one night when I asked him about it. "I swear I've never seen it before. Though, I can say that I wish some other part of your body twitched. It could be kind of fun." Funny, isn't he?

"What has you so stressed out?" he asked.

"Oh, you know, waking up and wondering whether I'll play tennis with Brit or play polo with Teddy," I said, "shop at Bergdorf's or take a late lunch with Buffy. What do you think has me all stressed out? This contract we've been going over for weeks is going to drive me crazy."

David hadn't realized how bad things had gotten.

"It feels like we're negotiating a business deal," I said while David sat there stunned. "I hate it. Here we are talking about gas mileage and a baby in the same sentence. I just hate it! It turns my stomach and I can't do this anymore."

I couldn't tell from the look on David's face whether he thought I had totally lost it or if he agreed.

"It feels wrong," I wailed. "It just feels wrong. How are we ever going to explain this to our child?"

David, of course, didn't have an answer for that one. "I don't know, Michael," he finally said. "I don't know."

We sat in silence until David said, "Maybe this isn't such a good idea after all. Maybe we should have gone through with an adoption. At least that way we wouldn't be going through any of this. What is the agency doing about all of this?"

"Nothing," I said, "absolutely nothing; Michelle and I are so aggravated with them we could strangle them."

Now I was really losing it. All this work, time, and research, not to mention soul searching, answering personal questions, thinking and more thinking, and now we were thinking about changing our minds, again! Now David wasn't even sure if we were doing the right thing. What about Michelle? How would we find another perosn like her? *No way,* I thought. *No way is this going to fall through.*

Michelle picked up on our feelings right off the bat. "I hate to get into the 'business' part of this," she wrote in an e-mail, "but this is just one of those things that are necessary for a wonderful journey. We have to get through this. We just have to, so that the rest of the journey turns out okay."

I didn't see how we could have a wonderful journey if we were arguing over thirty-six cents a mile. Was I being petty? Was she? What frustrated us even more was there really wasn't anyone to ask. We knew of no one else who was either going through a surrogacy or had gone through one. To make matters worse, our agency seemed to have fallen off the face of the earth. We were completely on our own. The surrogate community seemed to at least have a network of support via the Internet—they could post a thread asking questions and get dozens of responses—but I couldn't find any such resource for intended parents. It felt as though we were in a screw-or-get-screwed type of situation, where both sides were clearly, and solely, looking out for themselves.

Finally, after several days, we made some progress. Michelle agreed to drop the insemination fees and the monthly allowance. However, she didn't mention the mileage, meaning it stayed. Was I bitter? You bet I was. I couldn't for the life of me let it go. I knew it was trivial. I knew in the grand scheme of things that it was silly to quibble over what would amount to be a couple hundred dollars. David and I mulled it over for several days and finally called our agency and demanded they give us some advice. That's what we had paid $10,000 for, after all.

Finally, our agency responded. "It's tricky," the director said. "This boils down to about two hundred fifty dollars spread out over ten months. What you have to ask yourselves is this: are you going to walk away from what is otherwise a good relationship over two hundred fifty dollars?"

It was a good question and fair. However, I felt it should have been asked to everyone involved. Why didn't someone ask Michelle that very same question? Was she willing to walk away from two great guys over thirty-six cents a mile? If anyone were going to ask her that question it would have to be us, as our agency wasn't going to touch the subject with a 400-foot pole. That's the thing about working with an agency. Surrogates have the impression, I think it's fair to say, that the agency only looks out for the intended parents, as they are the ones paying the fee. Not true. Not in our case, anyway.

I tried one last time to explain our feelings to Michelle in an e-mail, but I didn't get very far at all. "It sounds to me like you are having second and third thoughts," she wrote, "and maybe that you are not wanting to pursue surrogacy anymore. Or not right now?" she continued. "Or not with me?" It was another good question. It was another fair question. We just didn't know how to answer it. We didn't want to lose her. However, I couldn't wrap my brain around the fact that the signing of our contract came down to a matter of $250, when our entire journey would likely cost us in excess of $35,000.

I wrote another e-mail to Michelle, sensing that she may be feeling as though we were trying to take advantage of her. "I understand how people could very easily take advantage of their surrogate, but we aren't looking to do that. We've agreed to nearly every one of your fees, including compensation, C-sections, and multiples," I wrote, "but this gas mileage is something I can't resolve. We're trying to look out for you as much as we are trying to look out for ourselves.

It's just that asking for mileage is so business-like," I explained. "It reminds me of work. When I go on a business trip or drive somewhere that's business related I get reimbursed for gas mileage. It's also something that I don't feel comfortable being a friend and talking about."

"True," Michelle responded, "but I'm not going to the doctor's office for myself. I'm going for you. I'm going for your baby, not mine. I wouldn't have any reason to drive there if I weren't carrying your child. This won't be my baby; it will be yours."

Wow, I thought. *You can't sum it up more than that.* This was going to be our baby, not hers. We would walk away from this entire process with a baby of our very own.

However, we were still getting nowhere. Michelle was as adamant as David and I. Neither side was willing to reach a compromise. As a last resort, I actually started looking online again and put a call in to our agency to let them know that we were very close to walking away and wanted to continue looking for someone else.

Then, one day at work, a colleague asked me how things were going. "Good, I think," I managed to mutter but obviously not nearly as excited as I had been.

"Well," she said, "you have no reason to be down. You're going to have a baby. You are going to be a father. You are very lucky to have found her, you know. I mean, she's desperate for money and you're desperate to have a child, so it's a match made in heaven."

Her statement hit me like a ton of bricks. That's it, I thought. That's what it is. That's what's bothering me. I hated what she had said about both sides being desperate. It wasn't the first time I had heard it, but this time it wasn't said in a mean way, nor was it meant that way. I knew it was just her way of saying that we both wanted something. Are David and I desperate? Is Michelle desperate? So, I wrote Michelle one last e-mail.

"I work full-time, Mike," she wrote, "so no, I'm not desperate. I don't need the money. I don't even want the money. I'm going to use it to make my family happy. I won't be spending it on myself. I'll be spending it all on them."

After another night of not sleeping and waking up drenched in sweat, teeth hurting and my eyelid twitching away, I realized something else. I had become a "yes" person. You know, the kind of person who says yes to everything and anyone just to keep the peace and not make waves? I had become that person. If someone wanted something I would say yes, even though what I truly wanted to say was no. I would just stew about it later. It was much easier than standing up for what I needed or what I wanted. The best part of this arrangement was people liked me. They didn't respect me, but they liked me. Everyone else seemed to be calling all the shots. We'll do this, or that. I'll do this if you do that. It seemed endless. It also seemed like I had no control over any aspect of my life. I kept asking myself if I was really desperate to have a child. Did I want a child? Yes. Was I willing to go above and beyond to have a child? There was no other way. But, was I desperate? Would I do anything? No.

After thinking more and more about what Michelle had said about all of this being done for our child, not hers, it finally sunk in. This was going to be our child, not hers. There just wasn't anything more to say, or ask. It just became excruciating to talk about it anymore. The thought of going back to the drawing board, posting another ad, talking to more surrogates, more phone calls, more small talk, and more questions seemed ridiculous.

It also occurred to me that even if we were lucky enough to find another surrogate to work with, we would still end up going through all of this again. In short, we would probably end up quibbling over the very same things with a different person. It is standard that surrogates receive gas mileage. We were lucky in some regards that she didn't live farther away from her doctor's office. We were also fortunate in that this wasn't a gestational surrogacy where we would be paying expenses, like gas mileage, for two people, the surrogate and the egg donor. Not to mention the fact that we liked Michelle. We wanted to work with her, not someone else. In the end, David and I decided that it just wasn't worth it to argue anymore. It certainly wasn't an argument we were going to win.

With the contract phase nearly over, we came to another conclusion, and it really bothered us. Like it or not, surrogacy is part personal and part business, at least the contract phase. It was a very tough conclusion to come to. I knew that David and I couldn't have children of our own, and therefore we had to take some extraordinary measures to have a child, whether it was through an adoption or surrogacy. Neither route was easy or cheap. However, having a baby, or bringing a child into this world, didn't seem right if it was going to be even remotely like a business deal. I had to come to terms with it. Negotiating terms, fees, and prices was part of the process. I just had to find a way to accept it. The fact that we liked Michelle so much made it easier. We were truly enjoying writing e-mails back and forth and were still getting to know each other. Plus, we had made it through one of the most difficult and stressful times of our entire journey. We had made it through it all by doing it all ourselves, and we had come out of it relatively unscathed. The bottom line was that we were starting to love her and she, in turn, was starting to love us.

In the end, yes, there is money involved. One thing that gave us peace of mind was knowing that no one was being taken advantage of. *Michelle wasn't going to come out of this independently wealthy,* I thought to myself, *but she is being reasonably compensated.*

We moved on. I started doing yoga and listening to meditation tapes to relieve some of my stress, but the sleepless nights were far from over. Over the next few weeks we talked on weekends and exchanged e-mails while Michelle filled out more questionnaires and had a phone-in psychiatric evaluation. "What a joke that was," she commented later. "The questions that they asked were just silly and not related to surrogacy at all!" The test is known as the MMPI. It was long, some 500 questions as I remember, and strictly multiple choice. We were sorry to hear that it was a "joke" as Michelle said, as we had paid to have it done and it seemed to be a complete waste of time. The more we thought about it, the more we realized that very little psychological evaluating was done on either side. We could be psychotic for all Michelle knew, and so could she. Not the best feeling in the world to have when you're about to try and get someone pregnant. At least with an adoption, a home study was performed. With surrogacy, there is no such thing. You pretty much base your decision on the surrogate's profile and conversations with them. Some agencies, unlike ours, I would later learn, conduct thorough background checks including credit history and criminal records. "If we ever do this again," David said, "and it's with a different surrogate, we'll see if we can have them go to some type of counseling—in-person counseling, that is—even if it's just a visit or two. The intended parents should have to do it also." I couldn't agree more. There should be at least some sort of unbiased party involved that can speak with both parties and give his or her opinion.

In the meantime, I needed to have bloodwork done and be tested for sexually transmitted diseases, including HIV and hepatitis. With contracts finally signed and behind us, we started planning a trip out to Nevada. We also had to start figuring out how we were going to get my sperm and Michelle's egg to shake hands, as it were. We weren't sure exactly how just yet, but one thing we did know was that it wasn't going to be easy.

Mike, David, Michelle,
and FedEx Make Three?

Journal Entry, November 2002
Okay, I knew this getting pregnant thing wasn't going to be easy,
but give me a break. We've had to order these kits through mail
of all things. Then I have to go do my thing, put it in a vial, put
egg yolk in with it, and ship it off. Worse than that, it has to be
done so fast! How am I ever going to explain this to our kid
someday? Well, you see, dear, we ordered a kit through the mail
and Daddy did his thing and then we sent it off to Nevada on a
FedEx truck! That, my little dumpling, is how you were con-
ceived. Holy crap!

The flight to Reno seemed like it was taking forever. I even resorted to reading the in-flight magazine to keep myself occupied.
Talking to David wasn't going to work because he was sound asleep
for most of the flight. Don't you hate when people can sleep anywhere, anytime, and through anything? Funny how David would
wake up the minute the food-and-beverage cart got about two rows
away from us, though.

My mind was racing. What if she doesn't like us? What if she
doesn't even show up? What if she got to thinking about things and
decided she wouldn't work with us if we were the last gay couple on
earth? I knew that I was driving myself crazy. For all I knew, Michelle
could be, and probably was, thinking the exact same things.

The plan was for Michelle, James, and their two kids to meet us at
the arrival gate. We didn't exchange what we would be wearing or
anything like that, but we had exchanged pictures.

So, we got off the flight and walked into the smoke-and-slot-ma-
chine–filled airport, but there's no sign of her. My heart was absolutely racing. What would I say? Hello? No, I couldn't just say hello.

It's nice to meet you? You're looking swell! What the hell would I say? With thoughts racing through our heads, we made our way to baggage claim but still saw no sign of her. All the while I'm thinking to myself, *Don't panic, there's no reason to panic.* Not yet, anyway. Of course, I was thinking all the worst possible scenarios, but didn't dare share them with David. Trying to spot Michelle was going to be like finding the proverbial needle in a haystack, as you would have thought they were giving flights away to Reno based on the sheer number of people in that airport. We plodded on. At one point David dared to ask if we could stop for something to drink. "You want something to drink right now?" I bellowed. "There's no time for drinking right now. We can't do that. We've got to find Michelle!" Boy, did I get a look from him after that; let's just say thank God looks can't kill. Then, just as we were starting around a corner, I spotted two red-faced adults hurriedly pulling two lagging kids behind them as they dodged their way through the myriad of people. All six of us came to a complete and total dead stop in our tracks. It had to be her.

"Michelle?" I asked.

"Mike!" she said. We hugged and cried all at once.

"Oh my God," she said, "you have no idea how scared we were that we missed you."

"I'm just glad you're here and we found each other," I said, while continuing to hug her. Michelle remarked how much taller I was than she had thought. Better that than thinking I was fatter than I looked.

"Wow!" all of us exclaimed at nearly the same time.

"You made it! You made it," she said over and over again.

"You did, too!" I said as we stood back in disbelief.

"Wow!" we all said again with a laugh. We had managed to find one another despite having the odds stacked against us. I can't remember what we talked about as we made our way to the rental car desk. The kids were beautiful, fair-haired, and blue-eyed. They seemed to sense how exciting it all was for us.

So what was it like meeting Michelle face-to-face for the first time? It was fun, stressful, sometimes strange, but amazing; you name it. It was every single emotion rolled into one. After renting our enormous minivan (you know, the kind you hate to get stuck driving behind), we headed off for four days of quality get-to-know-you time. Our hotel, or "resort" as they called it in the brochure, was less than a mile away from their apartment, which meant we had some fun day trips and lots of time spent together. David actually did most of the talking, as I played with the kids. David's a lot better than I am about small talk.

"We're not quite done unpacking," Michelle said as we entered their newly rented apartment. "We don't generally use plastic buckets as dining room chairs!"

We all laughed.

The kids were wonderful to spend time with. It was actually fun to watch a brother and sister so close in age stick things up each other's noses. David and I were both blown away by how well behaved they were. We were even given the honorary tour of their bedrooms and begged repeatedly to play the latest Xbox games. Michelle and James worked different shifts, which made it hard on their relationship, I imagine, but the kids benefited from getting their full, undivided attention, and it showed. We ate, we shopped, talked, went to the state fair in Reno, just hung out, and talked some more. Strangely enough, it didn't feel the least bit uncomfortable for any of us. Seeing Michelle, despite what we had gone through during the contract phase, was like seeing an old friend. We were all at ease around one another, including James and the kids.

"Is Mommy going to carry a baby for you and Dabid?" Michelle's daughter asked while we were playing with her vast assortment of undressed Barbie dolls. Michelle chimed in to let us know that her daughter was having trouble saying her Vs.

"I hope so," I said with a laugh. "I really hope so. So, what do you think of all of this?" I asked.

In typical kid fashion you could see the wheels turning behind a huge smile, and then she blurted out, "I think it's cool!"

After a little more playing with Barbie she asked, "Are you and Dabid brothers?"

"Well," I said, "no, we're partners." She wanted to know if that was like Barbie and Ken.

"No, not quite," I said. "We're more like your mom and dad."

"But you're boys, silly," she said with excitement.

"Yep, we're boys and we live together, eat together, and share our lives together just like you and your mom, dad, and brother. We're a family just like you, except I don't have a brother."

She gave it another moment's worth of thought before coming clean about her brother: "He's okay, for a boy."

"Well," Michelle said from across the room, "you've certainly passed the kids test!"

Michelle was as friendly and bubbly in person as she was in her e-mails and on the telephone. James couldn't have been nicer. We ended up going to the Nevada State Fair, in Reno, and to watch one of James's ballgames the night before we left. What was so amazing about the whole trip was that there didn't seem to be any pretense at all. It was just an incredible feeling to be meeting the woman who would be the birth mother of our child and her family. It was just an incredible, amazing, and exciting feeling.

David and I managed to sneak away for a day alone in nearby Lake Tahoe, California, and the next day we all headed back in to Reno. We talked about everything and anything, not just surrogacy and having a child. That's what made the trip even nicer. It wasn't a pressure trip, or a feeling of being measured up and down. Our month's worth of phone calls and e-mails had helped more than I knew.

Before long we had to say good-bye. The trip seemed to come and go faster than I could have imagined. Just before we walked out the door Michelle let us know that she would be switching over to James's insurance. It was something that she had told us about weeks ago while she and I were exchanging e-mails. Right now, she had her own insurance through her job, but explained that she was going to be switching over so that they were all on the same policy. It made perfect sense. It would cost us an additional monthly payment once we were pregnant, but we needed that insurance coverage badly.

"Not a problem," I said, "as long as this company covers surrogacy."

"Well," Michelle explained, "the wife of one of the guys that James works with is a surrogate mother for a straight couple out here and her insurance has been covered all along."

It would take several weeks, if not a month or so, for the change to take effect, and in the meantime, Michelle still had her insurance through her job.

Right before we walked out the door I asked her how we were going to do this. "You mean get pregnant?" she asked with a giggle. "Well, I think we should do home inseminations. It would be easier and a lot cheaper than going to a clinic. What do you think?"

"I'm fine with it," I said, "as long as you know what you're doing, because I don't have a clue!" Leaving was really, really hard to do.

We had to say good-bye the night before, as our flight left at some ungodly time in the morning, plus they both had to get to work. We promised to write the minute we got back to let her know that we had made it back safe and sound. The kids didn't want us to leave. I don't think Michelle wanted us to leave, either.

So, get this. Michelle had already been tracking when she was ovulating for the past several months. During our visit, we decided that we'd give inseminations a try in September. But, guess what? We didn't have to fly back out to Nevada, we just sent it via FedEx! That's right. FedEx. We ordered this special sperm-shipping "kit" from a company called Bio-Tranz. My sperm was put into a little vial with an egg-yolk buffer and an ice pack. The egg yolk was something for my little guys to eat, and the ice pack would keep them cold. Not exactly romantic, is it? However, buying the kit was a lot cheaper than airfare. We found out on the following Tuesday afternoon that Michelle was ovulating the very next Saturday, which meant I had to get in gear and get the kit out to her Friday afternoon. We also had to pick up my car, go to the bank, and pick up a new pair of glasses that David had been obsessing about. It was far from our typical day.

"Okay," David said, "you better go do your thing; it's getting late." There was no way I was going upstairs alone to masturbate.

"We can't do that," I said. "What would we tell our kid someday when he or she asks how Daddy and Dad made a baby?"

We both headed upstairs for what had to have been the quickest quickie for both of us.

Twenty minutes later, we're standing in line at FedEx holding onto my shipment for dear life, and I hear the clerk ask the man ahead of us, "What's in the box, sir?" I thought to myself, *If she even thinks of asking me that question I'm gonna scream like a girly man and run like hell.* Baby or no baby, I refused to tell some nosey FedEx clerk that my semifrozen, yolk-eating sperm was in the damn box and that it had to get to Reno by 10 a.m. tomorrow morning or I'd be back next month with two boxes and a crate of eggs.

Michelle received the package the next day, defrosted it, and did the insemination. She e-mailed later and said that when everything thawed it was "messy, yucky, and runny." *Well,* I thought, *if we have triplets I don't have to worry about names now, do I?*

Right off the bat, Michelle didn't think round one had worked and she was very upset. "I'm sorry, guys," she wrote, "I don't think it worked this time. I know it's still too early to tell, but I just don't think it worked and I'm not sure what else we can do." I got on the phone immediately. "We'll keep trying," I said. "We'll just keep trying." I had recently gone online and done some research about infertility, and I shared what I had learned with Michelle. "Do you know there is only like a twenty-five percent chance that a normal, healthy, average couple will get pregnant every time they try?" "Geesh," she laughed. "No, I didn't know that." "Yeah," I said, "and that's with straight sperm that have a clue what they are doing." We briefly talked about going to a fertility clinic, but finding a clinic willing to inseminate a surrogate was difficult, let alone for a gay couple. I tried to cheer her up by asking her to help "my guys" along a little. After all they've been through! They were probably like "La-tee-da, la-tee-da. We're swimming. We're swimming." Then, they see the egg! "What the hell is that? Backstroke! Backstroke!" She chuckled and seemed to relax. She was probably thinking if she didn't laugh I was going to get on a plane and arrive at her front door buck naked, demanding we do it "right" this time. "If it doesn't work this time, Michelle," I said, "then we'll try it again in another month."

So, we sat back and waited. It's called the 2WW, or two-week wait. It doesn't sound all that bad, but trust me, it's the longest two weeks you'll ever spend waiting. Michelle promised to not pee on any of her sticks until at least ten days had passed. I bet her she couldn't wait. I never did find out if I won that bet or not.

"Well, David," I said, "we might be pregnant. Let's just hope on their wedding day that our kids won't turn to me and say, 'Thanks for taking me down forty miles of bad road, Dad.' By that time, though, I'll be in my seventies and I can reach back and turn the volume down on my hearing aid. God knows, you'll probably be running around yanking carnations out of all the floral arrangements." David hates carnations.

Michelle had been saying that she was having "symptoms" of being pregnant. The only way to know for sure was to have a blood test done. The test confirmed what she had expected at the start: she wasn't pregnant. I felt terrible for Michelle. "Wouldn't you know," she said, "I got the call from the doctor's office at work. I broke down in tears in front of everyone."

Despite saying that we weren't, we were all very disappointed. Come to find out, the adults weren't the only ones feeling that way.

"My daughter was asking about the baby in my tummy tonight," Michelle said with her trademark giggle, "then she said that there wasn't a baby in there. I told her no. Not this time. But I did tell her that when there is we have to go buy baby clothes. You won't believe this, Mike," she went on, "but she looked at me and said that we weren't going to be keeping this baby because it's for Mike and Dabid."

I had promised myself I wouldn't get too excited while we were waiting, but I did. It was our first attempt and I knew that there was a very good chance that it wasn't going to happen. David had said early on that he didn't think it worked, and so did Michelle, but I still had my hopes up.

The weekend before, I had gone to one of my favorite places in the world: the bookstore. First I headed to the antiques and collecting aisle, but in order to get there I had to walk down the baby book aisle. Two hours later I found myself standing in line holding an *Italian Renaissance Craft Book* and *The Idiot's Guide to Having a Baby*.

"Congratulations!" the clerk said. "When is she due? Or did your wife already have the baby?"

"Hell," I said sheepishly, "I didn't expect to be buying baby books today. My partner and I aren't sure just yet if we're pregnant. As a matter of fact, he's probably wondering what the hell happened to me. My partner is like that sometimes, you know?" Nice, I thought. I'm standing here cursing like a truck driver while talking about having a baby with my partner. Do you think she had noticed that I had used the word partner fifty times in one sentence? If she did, she didn't bat an eye. In fact, she couldn't have been nicer.

"Good luck," she said with a huge smile, "and congratulations again!"

Needless to say, I kept my nose buried in the baby book while the craft book became a nice bedside coaster. In no time I knew more about baby barf and baby poop than I ever wanted to. I also put a call in to our agency. Amazingly, they returned the phone call pretty quickly. I wanted to know if we should be doing anything differently.

"You have to bombard the egg," the agency advised me. "When that egg drops you want all the sperm to be right there waiting for it. You literally have to bombard it. Attack it."

"That's a nice visual," I said, "kind of like kamikaze sperm?" All I knew was that if I were that egg, there wouldn't be a chance in hell that I'd ever drop. They'd have to come and get me. Following the advice from our agency sounded simple enough, but in reality it wasn't going to be nearly as easy. So, on to round two of trying to get pregnant.

> *Journal Entry, November 2002*
> *I'm trying not to get discouraged. We've only tried once, but I had my hopes up way too high. Everyone did, at least I think. It didn't help that Michelle kept thinking she was having symptoms. It's just this ovulation schedule and trying to predict it. It's proving to be more difficult that any of us thought. Thank God we aren't paying a couple of hundred dollars a clip! We'd be broke!*

By the time we found out when Michelle was set to ovulate, we had one day to get everything ready. Yes, just one day. But do you think I had ordered the Bio-Tranz kit ahead of time? Not a chance. If we were to do three inseminations over three days, we had to get my swimmers, as they had come to be known, out the door by Thursday and delivered to Michelle's door first thing Friday morning.

Let the drama begin. FedEx was supposed to deliver the kits Thursday afternoon. The plan was that I would come home on my lunch hour, do my thing, and then ship it off to her. But when I got home, there was no box, just a "Sorry we missed you" note. I freaked out, but I got on the phone and found out where the kits had ended up, then jumped back in the car, picked up the box at the FedEx office, raced back home, did my thing, put everything where it belonged, ice and yolk and all, and then raced back to work. All of that within my lunch hour! Not bad, huh?

Like it or not, my swimmers would have to sit out in the lobby of where I work waiting for the FedEx guy to come along a couple of hours later; but it wasn't over yet. I had to repeat the process on Friday, but this time I had to work off-site, which meant I couldn't come home for lunch. So, I decided that I would do my thing in the morning while at home, and then take the box to work with me once again. The alternative would have meant going into the men's room with my little kit and going at it. Things were going really well, until I made the turn into the parking lot at work and happened to look in the rearview mirror into the backseat. In nice, big, bold red letters I could see the words "Human Semen Shipping Container" written along the sides of the box. I panicked. There was no way I could leave that box with that written all over it out in the lobby at the TV news station without it being that night's top story on the evening news. So, I pulled over and started scratching off the labels with my fingernails. It wasn't working. That's when I resorted to using my car keys. Desperate times call for desperate measures. In no time at all there were cardboard shavings all over the floor and a deeply marred box was ready to go wait for FedEx.

While daddy worked away, the box sat out in the lobby.

Everything was going well, despite my near heart attacks whenever someone went near it. I kept waiting for someone to pick that box up and shake it up and down and all around trying to figure out what the heck was in there. Worst-case scenario was that my already stressed-out little guys would have to endure some rattling and rolling. *They're survivors,* I thought. Then, all day long, I had to listen to a co-worker complaining about how stressed out she was that she couldn't find her pair of scissors. Someone had borrowed them and failed to return them. This continued on the entire day. And I thought David obsessed over things. All the while I'm thinking, *Honey, you don't know stress. My sperm is sitting out in the damn lobby in a scratched-up cardboard box and you're stressing out about a pair of scissors? You don't know stress.*

Five o'clock came and out the door my frightened little swimmers went, but not before being banged up against the door, dropped on the floor, then tossed, no, thrown, into the back of a truck. But wait, there's more!

Friday night while watching television, it dawned on me that in order to do three inseminations we had to get a shipment out on Saturday, for Sunday delivery. Did I order enough kits? Are you kidding me? There wasn't time to panic, because I had to think fast, really fast. David was at work, so I was flying solo. All I could think of was that if I didn't have a shipping box, I would have to make one myself. I could do it myself, right? It's just a box with ice and stuff in it, after all. So, I bolted out of bed, ran over to a local pharmacy and bought some ice bags, then drove over to a craft store. After running around in circles trying to think of what I was going to use to keep "my stuff" and the egg yolk insulated, I spotted some Styrofoam containers. Eureka! Not any old containers, no, I could only find cone-shaped forms. Now what? *Well,* I thought, *just start from the bottom and hollow out the middle.* The vial of gook would fit in there nicely, then I can use the hollowed-out part as kind of a plug to keep everything nicely chilled! Martha would have been so proud. That's when it dawned on me that in my rush to get out the door I hadn't put my shoes on. There I stood in aisle three of Jo-Ann Fabrics in my dirty, beat-up old slippers.

So, after only a few hours and almost dropping my swimmers on the kitchen floor, the box was neatly wrapped, packaged, labeled, and ready to go. That's when it dawned on me that FedEx didn't deliver on Sundays. Damn! Damn the FedEx! After several desperate phone calls and learning that I could get it there overnight on a Sunday if I paid several hundred dollars, I had to resign myself to the fact that, like it or not, we would have to settle for two inseminations, rather than three.

"Who's the one that gets carried away with the packing tape?" Michelle asked after getting her package Saturday morning. She probably assumed it was David.

"It was me," I said.

The following weekend, while waiting for Michelle to pee on more sticks, I ended up learning a very important lesson. We went to visit my parents, celebrate my thirty-eighth birthday, and see our twelve-year-old golden retriever, Ashley, in upstate New York. Ashley had been spending summers with my parents and had survived two prior bouts with cancer. None of us ever expected that we would be making the unbearable decision to have her put to sleep while we were there. The cancer had returned and Ashley was in pain. David and I, along with my father, stood right beside her while she passed on.

When we got back home, Mom said, "She waited for you. Ashley knew you were coming and she waited for you." It just about broke my heart because I realized that I had become so focused on having a child that I hadn't thought to ask how Ashley had been doing. I realized that having a child would be a gift, but that it couldn't become the sole focus of my life. It's a lesson I hope I never forget.

We were back in the two-week wait. Believe it or not, I found myself questioning whether I'd make a good parent only once or twice. A co-worker brought her bouncing blond-haired, blue-eyed, eleven-month-old son into work one afternoon, and a group of us gathered around and started making silly noises and talking in baby talk. Then, one of us, it wasn't me, reached out to grasp his tiny little pudgy hand. At that instant, junior let out a scream that would rival any diva.

"Oh," the baby's mom said, "you can't do that! Don't do that! He doesn't like it when you touch his hands!" We were all shocked, complete with eyes bulging out of our heads. I think I had my hands over my ears.

"You can't touch his hands?" a stunned onlooker asked.

"No," his mom explained. "He's never liked anyone, including me, touching his hands and sometimes even his feet. He just hates it. We don't really know why. He just hates it."

All I could do was stand there and think how this little tyke is neurotic and he's only eleven months old. Oh, the drugs that child would be on if I were his parent. Forget that—oh, the drugs that I would be on if I was his parent.

"I'm hoping it's just a phase he's going through," his frazzled mom explained. *If that's a phase,* I thought, *then that means there are more phases to come.* I don't know if I could deal with that. It's different when you visit someone with a baby. You know that it's only temporary. You can go home. When baby starts "fussing" or screaming, you can just hand him or her back over to Mommy and Mom, or Daddy and Dad, but the baby's parents can't. It's theirs! It's a life-long commitment and responsibility.

Later that same week I would learn that commitment and responsibility didn't just involve being a parent, but also involved trying to become one. Things had been very stressful at work, with lots of long hours. One night that week, after a particularly bad day, I stormed out of the office and into the parking lot. I called David and promptly told him of a decision that I had just made.

"I'm quitting," I said in a huff. "I can't do this anymore. I am quitting, that's all there is to it. Hello? Hello? Did you hear me? I'm quitting."

A surprisingly calm David said, "Yes, Michael, I hear you loud and clear. But here's the thing: we're trying to have a baby. Now, here you are calling me at nine-thirty at night saying that you want to quit your job?"

"Yes! Yes!" I said. "I'm quitting." I may have even stamped my foot on the ground for added drama.

"The problem with that," David said, remaining unshaken by my tirade, "is that we can't afford to have you quit your job right now. It's just not an option."

"Oh," I said. "It's not?"

"No," David said, "it's not."

"I'm quitting! I'm telling you, I'm quitting," I wailed.

"Michael, if you quit your job today," David repeated, "we cannot afford to have a child. Okay? It's just that simple. You cannot quit your job."

"Okay," I said and then proceeded to get back to work even though it was difficult to do with my tail between my legs.

Despite our efforts at becoming shipping experts, we learned in an e-mail from Michelle that we were on to round three. Yes, round three of trying to get pregnant. While Michelle, David, and I tried to figure out why we weren't getting pregnant, the reactions of others started pouring in. Most said, "I'm sorry. It will happen. Give it time." Others had questions such as, "Why the hell did you have to find someone so far away?" Then there was the eternal pessimist among all of us who said, "It's not going to work. You can't keep sending your sperm in a box to Nevada! That's just stupid."

The last one, though a little rough around the edges, had a point. We had already done three inseminations at $175 each and to no avail. "That's as much as an airline ticket," Michelle said. That got us thinking. Michelle had been tracking her cycles and our doctors agreed that doing the inseminations before, during, and after ovulation was the best bet at getting pregnant. So, what was going wrong? We started looking into different reasons, including using the kits to ship my sperm. The whole point in express mailing my sperm was to get it there as quickly as possible. But, by the time I could get the shipment out and she was able to do the inseminations precious hours were passing by. Michelle was already a mom, so how could it be her? So, that left me.

We thought it was time that I had a sperm count done to make sure everything was fine on my end. *How could it not be?* I thought to myself. It honestly didn't faze me until I read online that smokers tend to have lower sperm counts and slower-moving sperm—both of which can have a negative effect on trying to get pregnant. Yes, I was a smoker. It's not something that I'm proud of. In fact I went out of my way to not let people know that I smoked, since it's become such a hotly debated issue.

If FedEx wasn't working, what else was there? You probably wouldn't believe me even if I told you. But buckle up. A bumpy, very bumpy, ride lies ahead.

–4–

Not Quite Pregnant

Journal Entry, October 2002
I just got off the phone with David and can't believe what I just
heard. It's me. I'm the reason why we aren't getting pregnant! I
am so confused, hurt, and angry at myself right now. What the
hell are we going to do? What the hell am I going to do? What
will Michelle say when I tell her? I can't believe this. Everything
seems as if it's going to fall apart. What have I done? I don't
want to tell her. I can't tell her. I'm scared to death that she's go-
ing to leave if I do. But I have to tell her. I just don't know how.

So, FedEx wasn't working; it was time to figure out how to get
pregnant without FedEx, Styrofoam boxes, and egg yolks. Things
were going along pretty well. E-mails were going back and forth and
Michelle kept tracking her cycles. In one of her e-mails Michelle suggested that we try doing the inseminations in person. Yes, you read
that right, in person. We would fly out to Nevada, and it looked as if it
was going to be before Thanksgiving. No more shipping boxes across
the country and hollowing out Styrofoam cones. We would still do
the home-insemination routine, but this time there weren't going to
be semifrozen vials and egg yolks. It would all be done "fresh."

Oh, and the "we" wasn't David and I, as you might have assumed.
It was actually my mother and I. Believe me, it wasn't my idea. It was
David's. He wasn't so keen on my going out there alone—he couldn't
go because of work—and my mom wanted to show her support in any
way she could.

The look on a friend of mine's face after I told him that my mom
was heading to Reno along with me was priceless. "How are you going to do that?" he asked. "How are you going to handle doing that
with your mother around?" All I could do was laugh and say, "I don't
know."

While I made travel plans, Michelle was busy peeing on sticks, tracking her cycle, and waiting to ovulate. We even bought her a high-tech electronic predictor kit. It was kind of like a palm pilot gizmo but with a pee stick attached to it. The only hitch was that we couldn't book our flights until Michelle started to ovulate, but we made as many other reservations as we could.

"I can't wait to meet your mom," Michelle said after I told her of our plans. "She's going to play a very important role in the child's life, and I can't wait to meet her." We even made plans to go trick-or-treating with the kids on Halloween.

However, our plans were about to take a complete left turn. We had hit another unexpected setback. This time, though, it was all because of me.

The very next weekend David called from the hospital. The results of my sperm analysis were back. I knew immediately from the tone of his voice that something was wrong: terribly wrong.

"I don't want to tell you this," he said, "because you're going to be very upset." After repeatedly asking him what was wrong, David went on to explain that the test results were good, overall. My count was okay. Motility, morphology, and some other "ologies" were all okay.

"So then please tell me what's wrong," I pleaded.

"Well," David said, "there's a problem and we're not sure what it is yet. Some white blood cells also showed up in the sample and that means that there's some sort of problem."

"What kind of a problem?" I asked. "What does that mean?"

"You've got to calm down, Michael," he said. "We really don't know. All I do know is that white blood cells," he tried to explain, "mean that there is some type of an infection or inflammation. As long as they are present, your sperm can't function properly."

I still couldn't wrap my brain around what David was saying. In my mind, if the sample was good, then what difference did it make that there were white blood cells present? There was a very long pause before David said, "There's something else I need to tell you. Okay?"

"Tell me," I begged. "You've got to tell me."

"Michael," David explained, "we probably aren't going to be able to have a child until we take care of this infection, or whatever it is, because Michelle isn't going to get pregnant as long as white blood cells are present."

It was the absolute last thing that I expected to hear. My heart sank and my mind went into overdrive. It was seven o'clock at night and I would have to wait until the next day to get some answers. It took an hour or so before I could get up off the floor, collect my thoughts, and figure out what to do. I was devastated, confused, angry, and tired, very, very tired. With all the stress of the past few weeks I hadn't been taking care of myself at all. I hadn't been getting rest, sleep, or any kind of relaxation, and after not smoking, I started smoking all over again. I have since quit smoking for good, but it was the hardest thing I've ever done.

I knew that the first thing I needed to do was cancel our trip out to Nevada, indefinitely. What I didn't know was how to tell Michelle, let alone my family and friends. Telling Michelle was going to be very difficult, as I knew that she would have a million questions; but they were questions that I couldn't answer. My absolute biggest fear was that she wouldn't work with us anymore. We had done two rounds of inseminations and weren't getting pregnant, now this.

"She's going to move on to another couple," I told David on the phone later that night.

"Well," he said, "we have to tell her. There's no choice. If she wants to move on, then she wants to move on; but I can't believe that she'll do that."

"But, it's been such a waste of her time," I cried to David. "She could have been working with some other couple and be well on her way right now."

"Michelle has invested a lot of time and effort into this, Michael," David said, trying to reassure me. "I'm sure she'll be upset, but not that upset as to say that she won't work with us anymore."

"What if . . . ?" I asked. "Does this mean that I could have given it to Michelle?"

"No," David said, "don't even think about that."

I knew that I had to tell her. I'm embarrassed to admit it, but I didn't want to call her and talk to her on the telephone. I was upset and I didn't want to upset her so I sent her an e-mail. Not even fifteen minutes passed and the phone rang. It was Michelle. "Call me," she said on the message. "Please, just call me. No matter what time it is, please, call me." Before she hung up she said, "I just need to know if you are okay."

She sounded scared and confused and needed to talk to me as much as I needed to talk to her. I picked up the phone and called her back. The first thing she asked was if I was okay. "I wish I could tell you what was going on," I said, "but I can't. I'm not sure myself." I went on to tell her that one of my biggest fears was that she would become so frustrated with us that she would want to move on and help another couple. "I don't know how long this is all going to take," I said. "It could be months." Michelle said she just wanted me to be okay. All I could do was promise her that David and I would try to get to the bottom of what was causing the problem. I spent the next few days on the telephone talking to our doctors and ended up being put on medication. They were horse-sized pills that I had to take twice a day for an entire month. Michelle was patiently waiting to find out the results.

Her e-mails during that time were some that I will never forget. "I would wait for you guys forever," she wrote in one. "Well, maybe not forever, but for as long as it takes." In yet another she wrote, "I seriously have no regrets working with you guys. Even if I have to wait a year, I will. And, I'll smile the whole time, because finally handing a little squalling ball of baby powder over to you and David will be worth every last second of it."

I had been suffering through a terrible head cold, so we waited two weeks for that to clear up and then went back for another test. I was still positive. White blood cells were still in the sample. "It could be the result of any number of things," one of our doctors said. "It could be that the infection wasn't treated as we had thought, and that your prostate has become inflamed as a result." A reproductive specialist added, "We should have waited a full month, if not longer, before testing again; sperm isn't generated that quickly."

We would have to wait until December at the very earliest to resume inseminations. Hopefully, the antibiotics would clear up the infection or inflammation. If not, I would need further tests to determine what was wrong. Accepting the fact that we would have to wait up to two months before doing any more inseminations was very difficult. Not knowing if the treatment would work was even more difficult. I was getting very, very scared, and Michelle picked right up on it. "You sound so stressed about this, Mike," she wrote in another e-mail, "but stressing out about it isn't going to help. Take your medication and have another test done. It's that simple. It will happen. We'll get pregnant. There's no rush."

> *Journal Entry, November 2002*
> *I can't eat. I can't sleep. All I do is lay there tossing and turning. I can't even focus on my job, and it's starting to show. This waiting for the test results is driving me crazy. What if I can't father a child? What if all of this has been for nothing? What if all of this time and energy, not to mention money, was for nothing? How can that be possible? Can God be so cruel? This is such a mess, just a complete and total mess. I can't believe that I got me, and David, into this.*

My main fear was wondering what if the very thing that I wanted so much in my life wasn't going to happen or wasn't meant to be. Then, another thought entered my mind. Depending on the results of the treatment, I might have to step aside while David went ahead with inseminations. Come to find out, I wasn't the only person thinking that. While out to dinner one night with a group of our friends, one of them asked, "Why don't you just let David try?" I honestly couldn't answer him. It didn't help that I had a mouthful of guacamole. "We'll see," David said. "It's too early yet, but we'll see."

It took me years to accept my feelings of wanting to have a child of my own. Now, while popping two pills a day for a month, I had time to think and ask myself how I felt about it. A friend of ours asked why having David's child would bother me so much. "It's completely selfish of me," I said. "I love David with all my heart, but I can't help but wonder if I would resent him or, worse yet, resent our child." My friend summed it up by saying, "It's kind of like a 'why not me' type of feeling isn't it?" "Yeah," I said. "It is."

Michelle wanted to know if we had a backup plan as well. "I totally understand," she wrote, "that you want to have a child of your own. It's completely understandable, so don't think you owe anyone, including me, an explanation." She was also wondering if David would step in and do the next round of inseminations in my place. "It's not important to me who goes first or second," Michelle wrote, "what matters here is that you guys deserve to be parents and it's going to happen. It will happen."

Part of me thought that I would love our child just as much if it were David's, but I've learned that I don't always act or behave the way I thought I would, let alone should. Emotions are funny, aren't they? Sometimes they get in the way of common sense and reason. You don't always want them, but you always have them, whether they are rational or irrational. I guess it all depends on how we deal with them. I wish I knew. Figuring it all out was going to take time and some more soul searching.

We had at least one option. We had talked about it before. I could have a sperm sample taken and stored at a reproductive clinic. The sperm would be washed, or cleaned, to take it down to its purist form and ensure that it is free of disease and gunk. However, it was an expensive and lengthy process. The sample would have to be quarantined for six months and the cost would run several thousand dollars. In the end, we decided that the best course of action was for me to keep taking the medicine and then take another test. I tried to remain in a positive frame of mind, but it was very, very difficult to do.

"Just be thankful you had the test done," my doctor reminded me, "as these things don't always have symptoms. Now you know. Now you can be treated and move on."

In the meantime, I was cheered up when I found out that our child was going to have more honorary aunts and uncles than I had ever imagined. Our friends had been truly amazing throughout all of this. I think they wanted us to get pregnant as much as we did. Our friends couldn't wait to start planning the baby shower, and my mom asked me one day if we had given any thought about whom we would name as godparents.

It was so difficult not to make plans and think about the future. I had already started thinking of what lucky people we would ask to be godparents long before my mother asked. I bit the bullet and asked two friends of mine. One jumped at the chance and said she would be honored. The other, as it turned out, was an atheist, or at least was having some serious doubts about organized religion, and couldn't figure out why I was asking people to be godparents before we were even pregnant. Leave it to me to ask an atheist to be the godfather of my child.

Plus, Michelle wasn't giving up easily. She was still tracking when she was ovulating and kept asking when we were coming out to do inseminations in person. We had spoken about trying again in December. However, along with December came the holidays. So, after talking about it we all agreed to try again, one way or the other, in early January 2003.

David and Michael, the intended fathers.

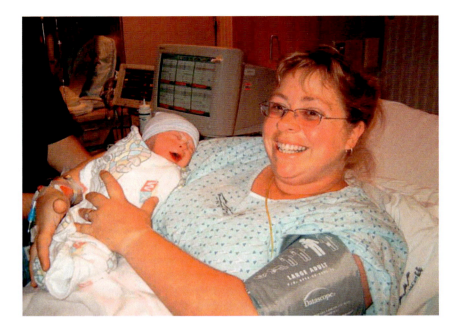

Michelle holding Lillian just minutes after she was born.

Grandmother and Grandfather Menichiello holding Lilly at her first Thanksgiving.

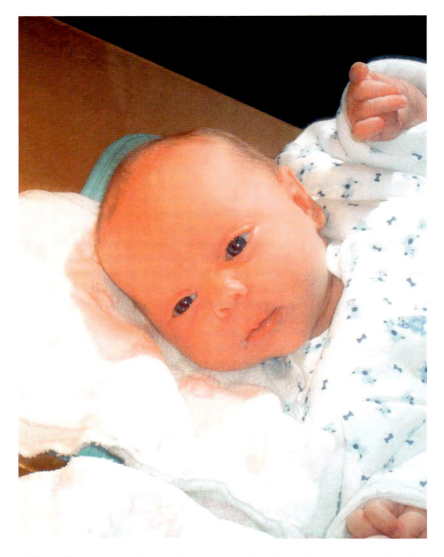

Lilly looking at her reflection in the mirror, already a diva at two months old.

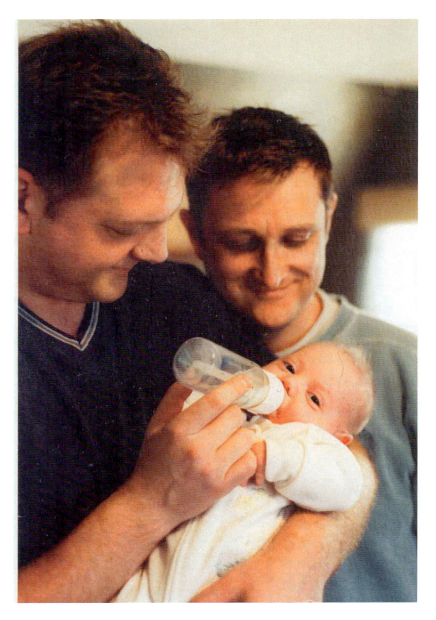

Two dads feeding Lilly at three months old. Notice the bags under my eyes!

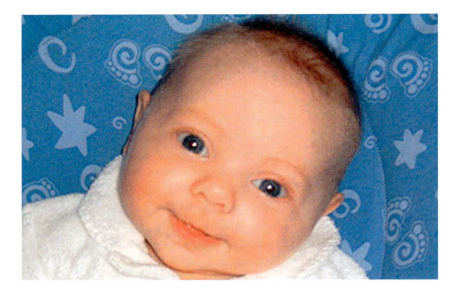

Lilly's ready for her close-up, at four months old.

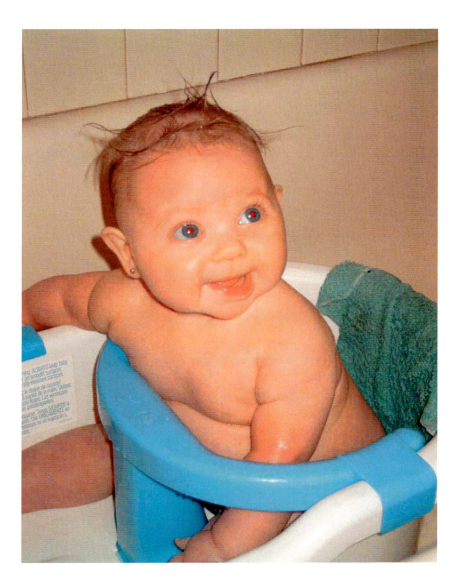

Splish-splash she's taking a bath in her new bathtub at six months old.

Lilly at two years old.

5

Conception Nevada

Journal Entry, January 2003
This morning, I found myself lying on the bathroom floor of our
efficiency trying to, well, rise to the occasion and do my thing.
But first, I had to drown out the sound of Mom doing dishes,
humming, and talking on the telephone in the background. Trust
me, it wasn't easy, but I did learn that turning the water on in the
bathtub, running water in both sinks, and turning on the over-
head fan worked just fine as distractions.

The phone rang at eight o'clock one Saturday morning. No one calls our house at eight o'clock on a Saturday morning, no one who knows us, that is. We're comatose. Through my delirium I could hear Michelle's voice on the answering machine. I turned to give David a nudge to answer the phone, but he had already left for work.

"Did you check your e-mails this morning?" Michelle's message started. "Well, if you didn't, or did, it doesn't matter. Call me as soon as you can."

That woke me up. I realized that with the three-hour time difference that it was only five o'clock in the morning in Nevada. My first thought was that something had to be wrong, otherwise Michelle wouldn't be wide awake and calling so early. I sprang out of bed and raced to the phone. Within two rings she answered the phone.

"Hi," a cheerful voice shouted over the phone. "Did you check your e-mails yet? Did you get my message?"

"No," I said, "and what are you doing awake so early?"

"Never mind that," she said with a giggle. "You definitely want to check your e-mail this morning."

I was still a little groggy, but with Michelle waiting on the telephone, I went to check my e-mail. Groggy or not, I could read and understand every single word she had written:

> Hi guys! I hope you're having a good weekend. I don't know what to tell you. I don't think we should plan on doing inseminations again in February. It's snowing here already and I don't know about driving up the mountains to Lake Tahoe for my doctor's appointments in the snow and ice. Plus, I don't know if it would be good for the BABY! Besides that, there's something else: Congratulations, Daddies! We're pregnant!

You might think that I would have jumped up and down or blown one of Michelle's eardrums out with a shriek, but I just started bawling. I couldn't believe what I had just read and kept reading it over and over again.

"Are you serious?" I asked a giggling Michelle.

"Yep," she said, "I'm dead serious. You're going to be a daddy!"

Much to my surprise, Michelle had already done two home pregnancy tests, and both had come back positive. "I did one last night because I just couldn't wait," she said, "and that came back positive. So, I was like, James, it's positive! The test came back positive! But he said, Well, we'll check again in the morning." That answered what she was doing wide awake at five o'clock in the morning!

"We did it! We did it!" Michelle said over and over again. By then all either of us could do was cry.

"I still can't believe it," I repeated in utter disbelief. "I just can't believe it."

"Well," Michelle said through tears, "it's true. It's true."

I had the news, but what about David? He had just left for work, so I frantically paged him. A few minutes later I answered the phone and a still-not-wide-awake David said, "Hi, Booger, what's wrong?" Booger is our affectionate, yet somewhat gross nickname for each other.

"Hi, Daddy," I said.

There was a long, long pause before reality set in. Then, sounding a little annoyed, he said, "Why are you calling me that, Michael?" Another long pause, then, "Oh, my God. Oh, my God! We're pregnant?"

"Yep," I said. "We certainly are. We're going to be daddies!" David was in complete and total shock.

"I can't believe it," he repeated. "You did it, Michael! You did it! You actually created a child!"

Anyone within earshot at the hospital heard the news. It was beyond a doubt one of the happiest days of my entire life. All the waiting and hoping and work had finally paid off. It was an unbelievable feeling.

"Was it confirmed?" David asked.

"No," I said, "Michelle is calling her doctor's office first thing Monday morning to set up an appointment, but she's had two home pregnancy tests and they both came back positive."

"Well," David said, "that's that! Those tests are ninety-nine percent accurate, so we're pregnant!"

I was bursting at the seams to tell everyone and anyone within a 400-mile radius that we were pregnant, but I hesitated. Why? Looking back, I worried that if I went around and told everyone before it was confirmed, I would then have to explain why we weren't pregnant if we got bad news. I had also heard that some people waited months before telling anyone their good news. I could last a few days, but not a few months.

Three days later Michelle called to let us know that her doctor's office had confirmed the great news. We were all just completely shocked. Nothing had gone according to plan and everything had seemed to be stacking up against us. First, she never officially ovulated, meaning her egg never dropped out of hiding to get its present: my sperm. That had us all feeling that it just might not have worked. Believe it or not, we even used the electronic pee-stick gizmo to determine when the egg was ready, but after it reached a high level, it froze.

"I honestly don't think either of the kids touched it," Michelle had said, after I realized she was keeping it on the bathroom counter. "They were told 'if you touch it that's the last thing you'll ever touch, with that hand anyway!'" Next, we tried over-the-counter ovulation predictors, but they didn't show any sign of ovulation either. Nevertheless, we plodded onward, as we were on a mission.

Then, there were the white blood cells stopping us from getting pregnant. The results of my second sperm test came back just two weeks before my mother and I planned to leave for Nevada. The antibiotics had worked: my white blood cell count had fallen as far down as it was going to go.

"I'm ecstatic," Michelle wrote in one of her daily e-mails after sharing the good news about my sperm test.

I wasn't as excited at first. It bothered me that the white blood cells hadn't completely disappeared, thanks to my continued smoking, and the actual sperm count had fallen as a result of the antibiotics. However, the infection had cleared, and my "swimmers" were still alive and well.

If that weren't enough, I received a frantic e-mail from her just days before our trip. "Oh my God!" she wrote. "I don't know what to do now! I have started my cycle three days early, which means I should ovulate three days sooner! What the heck is going on with my body?" That little bit of news left Mom and me scrambling to change all of our reservations including hotel, flight, and car. With all that done, we were finally ready to fly out to Nevada. It felt very strange to give David a hug and kiss good-bye, but he couldn't make the last-minute trip—so I had to make do.

I had a gut feeling all along that something was going to go wrong. All I could think of on the airplane were worst-case scenarios, from missing our plane and getting lost to my not being able to rise to the occasion for a full week.

I was right. Our flight to San Francisco landed just as our connecting flight to Reno was about to leave without us onboard. Mom and I ended up getting into a shouting match with a not-so-friendly airline employee. Our flights were on opposite ends of the airport, meaning there was no time for us to get from one gate to another. Finally, after running like crazy, dragging suitcases and coats, we arrived at the gate.

"You're late," the attendant said bluntly. "Your seats were given away."

I couldn't believe my ears. "We just landed on the other side of the airport," I said. "We're not standing here dripping in sweat from running to get a candy bar."

"We ran from one end of this airport to the other to make this flight," my exasperated mother added.

"Sir," the frazzled airline employee said, "if you and your wife don't calm down, I will have to call the police."

"She's not my wife, she's my mother," I said, "but it doesn't matter who she is because she's not too happy at the moment, and trust me, that's not a good thing."

Another airline employee appeared from the back. "Sir! You are being rude and abusive and if you don't calm down we're going to be forced to call the police!"

My mother and I just turned and looked at each other in amazement. "You made us run from one end of this airport to the next with our luggage, only to get here and be told you gave our seats away, which we bought and paid for, and you're threatening to call the police on me?" I said, not even believing I had just said it myself. I admit to being frazzled and tired, but rude and abusive? No way.

"The first thing she said to us," my mother interjected while pointing to a horrified clerk, "was 'you're late and we gave your tickets away.' Like we wanted to be late and we wanted to miss our flight. *That's* rude! *That's* abusive." I kept watching for one of them to make a sudden move toward the telephone to call the police, as my mother would have done a backflip over that counter and printed out our tickets herself before they knew what hit them.

"Call the cops!" I demanded. "Go right ahead and call them, but we have people waiting for us in Reno so I'd suggest you make it quick."

Needless to say, the cops weren't called and we were sent on our angry little way after being told that the next flight to Reno wouldn't leave for three hours.

"You'll be on standby," one of the clerks said as she handed us our boarding passes.

"Standby?" my mother asked. "If we miss that flight, how will we get to Reno?"

We both stood in amazement as the clerk said, "I suggest that you either walk or drive, but walking will take a while."

"I'll tell you who can take a walk and to where," my mother said as a parting shot.

With that the clerk turned on her heel and walked away. "I hate New Yorkers," we heard her say under her breath.

We passed the time by making phone calls to Michelle, letting her know that we were stranded. We also looked into renting a car and driving there, but the thought of driving for six hours wasn't too appealing. So we sat and ate and complained. Two hours later we were standing in line at security.

"Step aside, sir!" yet another friendly airline employee barked. I turned to ask my stunned mother to pass me my jacket, then she was promptly told to step aside. Our stay at San Francisco International Airport was quickly going down in our record books as the worst experience we'd ever had. We were frisked, patted down, and grilled as to where we were going and why.

"I'm going to Reno to meet a friend," I said nonchalantly. "We're trying to get pregnant."

"What does your wife think of that?" the security guard asked.

"She's not my wife," I said again, "she's my mother, but I think she'd take that as a compliment." There was no reaction. "Have we done something?" I asked and was promptly told to please be quiet or they would call the police. "You know," I said, "that's the second time someone has threatened to call the police on me today at this very same airport. Isn't that something? Who would have thought?"

"Sir," I was told, "please be quiet, or we will call for the police."

Nearly an hour had passed and we were finally seated on the plane, after waiting until the very last moment to board, that is. That's when I looked down at my ticket and noticed that a black line had been drawn all along the bottom of it. Mom's ticket had the same telltale marking. Then I remembered reading a bulletin from the ACLU about how airlines—following September 11—were color coding passengers they thought might be a security risk. After our run-in with the ticket agent, they must have marked our tickets without us realizing it.

"Damn," I turned to Mom and said, "we've been blacklisted by an airline!"

"After how they treated us, I'm honored," Mom said. "I'm deeply honored."

If you think our trip got better from there, think again. An hour later we landed in Reno, only to find out that our rental car had also been driven away by someone else!

We finally checked in to our efficiency hotel room twelve hours after leaving the East Coast. Needless to say, despite my efforts, there wasn't any way I was going to be able to salute and perform my duties that night. Inseminations were just going to have to wait until the morning.

So just how was I going to get Michelle pregnant? Good question. Believe it or not, with all the excitement and change in plans, Michelle and I hadn't even had time to think or talk about what we were going to do.

I did know that I would take a syringe and a sterile cup with me. I also knew that I would have to do my thing, get the end result into the cup, and then transfer it into the syringe. But wait, there's more! I also knew that Michelle and I then had to play beat the clock, as sperm don't like swimming around in a plastic cup, no matter if it was bought at CVS or Bloomingdale's. I had a grand total of fifteen to twenty minutes to transfer the semen, collect my things, grab the syringe, and race over to Michelle's. What's so stressful about that? I was so stressed out about it that I sat down with David before I left and asked his advice.

"You're going to have to just block everything out and concentrate, that's all," a reassuring David explained.

"How am I going to do this, though?" I asked. "How am I going to get, well, aroused, and do all of this with Mom sitting in the next room?"

David was silent. Silent until he started to laugh, that is. "I don't know, Booger," he said. "I honestly don't know."

So, it was time to ask Mom.

"Well," she said, surprisingly matter-of-factly, "I'll go for a walk or do something. I can work out or swim or something and give you your privacy, so don't worry about it."

Don't worry about it? I thought. *How am I going to do this?*

"What if you took some kind of magazines with you?" David suggested.

"Yeah," I said, "I'm going to take porno magazines with me to Nevada in front of my mother? I can't do that!"

"Well," David said flatly, "you'll just have to use your imagination." Boy, would I ever.

The next morning I woke up and showered, made coffee, got dressed, and called Michelle. "So, are you ready?" I asked, somewhat embarrassed.

"It's the perfect time," she said. "I'm the only one awake. James and the kids are sound asleep, so how soon can you get over here with the . . . the . . . you know . . . the stuff?"

Talk about pressure, I thought to myself.

"I'll do my best and hopefully be over there in about half an hour."

"Okay," Michelle giggled. "I'll be waiting!" Oh Lord, this wasn't going to be easy.

By then, Mom was wide awake and sitting with her cup of coffee watching television. We exchanged our good mornings and asked each other how we slept, and then I retreated to the bathroom to collect my thoughts and hopefully some sperm. Before I knew it I was lying on the bathroom floor of our efficiency trying to drown out the sound of Mom doing dishes, humming, and talking on the telephone while trying to arouse myself. Trust me, it wasn't easy. I thought about everything and anything, cursing myself for not at least taking a *TV Guide* in with me for some kind of inspiration. But, alas, I was spread out on the floor thinking and thinking. It didn't help matters that I kept pulling the condom off. No condom meant no sperm would be collected. The minutes quickly turned into nearly an hour. Finally, I had lift-off. I learned that turning the water on in the bathtub, running water in both sinks, and turning on the overhead fan did the trick. I also learned that *The View* had become one of Mom's most favorite of all morning programs—as I had to drown out the sound of Star Jones's voice, too.

Carefully, ever so carefully, I took the condom off and made my way over to the counter in the bathroom, where I would then go through the tedious process of transferring the contents to the cup, and from the cup to the syringe. We needed every last drop, so I always put the lid on the cup before I dared to move. This time, however, the unthinkable happened. In my nervousness I actually dropped the cup. Yep. That's right. I dropped it. No lid meant that my swimmers were set free by the thousands. Well, hopefully, I only lost thousands. What else could I do other than try and scoop most of them up and put them back. So, after all that work my "sample" was, well, there's no other way to describe it other than being miniscule at best. I immediately burst into tears. All I kept envisioning was Michelle coming to the door all happy and excited and then seeing this teeny tiny sample being handed to her. I could picture her either bursting into tears or demanding that I go back and do it again and again—not stopping until I had a respectable sample!

There wasn't time to dillydally. I had to get my act together, along with my composure, and get my stuff over there. I rushed out of the bathroom, stopping just long enough to tell Mom that I'd be right back and ask her what she'd like for breakfast. Then I made a mad dash for the truck. If only it were that simple. Things got worse. You see, in my excitement to get there, I didn't let the windshield defrost fully—I did have a little window to peak out of—and it helped me see the cement barrier as I drove over it. Of course, that sent my syringe of swimmers sailing across the truck. They landed down on the floor with a thud—albeit a little one. Rather than stopping, I gunned it. Michelle had already been waiting for over an hour, so my guys—or whatever was left of them—would just have to backstroke and amuse themselves for at least another five minutes until I got to Michelle's house.

"I'm so sorry about this sample," I said to Michelle while holding my head down. "First I dropped them on the floor, then I hit something in the parking lot and they flew across the truck. They probably have sperm brain damage by now."

"Don't worry about it," Michelle said while standing at the door with her hand out ready to grab the syringe at any moment and run. "It only takes one! Sorry, no time to chit chat, I've got work to do," she said with a huge smile.

My first attempt at live—in person—inseminations was dismal to say the least. I made my way to McDonald's to grab breakfast. I couldn't believe what I had just done. Did I really just masturbate on the floor of a hotel room, then drop off a syringe at Michelle's house so she could inseminate herself with whatever was inside? This was beyond bizarre. I got back to the hotel with breakfast in hand, and thankfully neither Mom nor I broached the subject of what had transpired that morning. That's how things would play out morning after morning, day after day for a total of six full days. I never saw so much action in my lifetime and, honestly, never want to again.

Journal Entry, January 2003
We've been doing these inseminations for three days now and I've become quite the pro at it, I must say. I'm a little weary, but I'm doing well. It's actually gotten pretty easy. I walk into the bathroom, plop down on the floor, do a little imagining, and voilà—instant sample. I did have a panic attack the other morning as I started wondering if anyone had seen me dropping off a syringe that I pulled from underneath my armpit every morning. I started thinking, what if I get there one morning and the cops come flying out from underneath the staircase and start yelling, "FREEZE!" It does look like we're doing something suspicious, you know? I still can't believe Michelle. I can't believe she's doing this for me. She's actually helping me become a father. Isn't that incredible? I just met her a few months ago and here we are trying to make a baby. It's unreal. How am I ever going to explain this to our child someday? This is all just so crazy.

There is something else that's a little weird. Michelle and James seem to be bickering a lot. Mom and I can't figure it out. But James keeps saying something about how we can take care of this and that when Michelle moves to New York to live with us. What? No, make that WHAT? What the hell is he talking about?

By the third or fourth day I was unstoppable. I had everything down to a routine, even the hardest part of getting everything slowly but surely in the syringe, right down to the very last drop. The funniest part, or strangest depending on how you look at it, was knocking on Michelle's door at the crack of dawn and making the hand-off. I could only imagine what her neighbors must have been thinking.

"Here you go," I said during the second drop-off. I was much happier with the contents of my second syringe. "Yell at them! Tell them what to do! Be firm, but not too forceful," I teased Michelle. She would say thanks, we would hug, and that was the extent of it. The third morning I knocked on the door expecting Michelle to be ready and waiting, but this time I heard a little voice say, "Hi there!" and I had to look down to see her daughter all bright eyed and bushy tailed. I could see Michelle doing a combination of acrobatic tricks and ballet to get to the door, but alas, she didn't make it there first!

While playing the slot machines with Mom I couldn't help but wonder what Michelle's kids and husband were thinking about all of this. One night we all went bowling and Michelle told me that her daughter in fact told everyone and anyone who would stop and listen that, "My mommy is going to carry a baby for Mike and Dabid."

An hour or so after our first insemination Michelle called the hotel room to let me know that everything had gone very well. Looking back, thank God it had, as it was on the very same afternoon that we think Michelle ovulated while we were all watching a carnival act at the Circus-Circus Casino. How appropriate is that?

Journal Entry, January 2002
Mom and I just got back from spending a wonderful day together. We've been spending most of our time with Michelle and the kids while James worked, but today we decided to go off by ourselves after I completed my morning mission. We ended up in Lake Tahoe. It was so amazing to spend the day with her. I'm so blessed. I'm just so truly blessed to have her in my life. Not only is she my mother, she's my friend—my best friend, second only

to David and my father. If someone had told me years ago that Mom and I would someday be spending the day together in California while I was trying to have a baby with a surrogate mother's help I would have smacked them. James is still making the comment about Michelle moving to New York. I can't figure out if he's just teasing, trying to be funny, or trying desperately to tell me something. Why don't I just ask him?

Michelle's husband handled it amazingly well. As a matter of fact, he handled it better than I did at first. I honestly don't know how Michelle did it. I truly don't. Between my samples ranging from tiny to overflowing, two kids running around the house, and company unexpectedly dropping by, you would have thought it was truly an immaculate conception. However, we had done it. Somehow, we had done it.

While on an afternoon trip to one of the casinos it dawned on me that James and Michelle seemed to be bickering a lot. They weren't knockdown, drag-out fights, of course, but there was something going on between the two of them despite their attempts to keep it low profile. I just couldn't put my finger on it. Not that David and I wouldn't have our spats, mind you. They were all David's doing, of course. But, at least three times during our trip James had said, "Well, when Michelle moves to New York to live with you guys you can take care of all that stuff." Neither Mom, nor I, knew what to make of it.

The first time he said it I was so taken by surprise that I thought he was joking. By the third time, though, I started feeling as though he was trying to tell me something. Was he dead-set against what Michelle was doing and threatening that if she went through with it she'd have to do it in New York? It couldn't be. Had he changed his mind? Were they arguing about the surrogacy? It just struck me as a very strange thing to say. James couldn't have been nicer or more welcoming the entire trip, but something was definitely up. Oddly enough, I never asked him what he was talking about. I had work to do, and if James had a problem with what we were doing, he was going to have to do a lot more than drop hints about it.

Just as Mom and I were headed out the door to go home, Michelle told me that there had been some major changes in James's health care coverage.

"Did you talk to these guys about the insurance thing?" James asked Michelle as she was giving me a hug.

"No," she said, "not yet."

"Well," he said, "you had better do it now."

Come to find out, James's health insurance policy through work had changed, and it wasn't for the better.

"Well, originally labor and delivery alone was going to cost about eight hundred dollars," Michelle said. "Now it looks like it could cost as much as thirty-five hundred dollars."

I couldn't believe my ears. James's company had revised their employee health plans so that they paid less and the employees chipped in more. The same exact thing had just happened to me at work.

"We'll look into it," Michelle said with a hug. "Don't worry about anything, okay? We'll look over the new policies and look into it."

On the way back home, I started to get a very sinking feeling in my stomach. Although Michelle knew of another surrogate who was being covered under the same insurance, I still had doubts, as we hadn't seen the actual policy. However, what was done was done. I was just thankful, very thankful, that we had insurance.

Our excitement over being pregnant lasted for several weeks, then something happened that we didn't expect. Michelle and I belonged to the same Web site for surrogate mothers, where we first read each others' ads. Subscribers could post messages and reply to those left on the "boards," as they're called. Sometimes, we posted a reply on the very same subject. Sometimes, as I was about to learn, that wasn't always a good idea.

While looking over the message boards one day, I found a thread that asked whether a surrogate would work with a couple who smoked. Being a smoker, and one who was trying to quit that very same week, I started reading the replies. Ninety-nine percent of the surrogates who responded said no, they would not carry a child for someone who smoked, or even lived with someone who smoked. It sounded a little harsh to me. Having been a smoker, the last thing I would do would be to expose my child, directly or indirectly, to cigarette smoke. Michelle knew that I smoked, as while David and I were visiting I lit up a cigarette while we were all outside at a park watching the kids play. She hadn't said anything. The only person who did say something about it was her son, who let me know that he thought what I was doing was "stupid and disgusting." So, imagine my surprise when I saw that Michelle had responded to the question and made it perfectly clear where she stood on the subject.

"No," her post said, "I absolutely would not be a surrogate for a smoker. It only takes a minute for something to happen," she explained, "while someone is outside having a smoke. It only takes a minute for something to go wrong. I would never work with a smoker or someone who even lived with a smoker."

First, I was stunned and felt judged. Then I got angry. We had gone through so much to get this far. We had put up with a lot of flack and dissention, not to mention one or two rude comments about our ability to be parents because we're gay, but not from Michelle. Now I was being told that I shouldn't be a parent because I smoke by our very own surrogate mother. I had had enough. Did I mention that I had quit smoking that very same week? For those around me, my quitting smoking was probably one of the worst experiences of their lives. I was far from a happy camper. I wanted to reply to the thread in the worst possible way. However, the last thing I wanted to do was to argue with Michelle in front of everyone else.

I couldn't understand the logic of some of the responses. I wondered if those same surrogates would work with a couple who didn't wear seat belts. What about people who got caught speeding? Or worse yet, what about someone pulled over for DWI? Should their children be taken away from them? It seemed ridiculous to me that a surrogate would judge and make the final decision as to whether someone should or shouldn't be a parent, when they in turn were being judged by others for even being a surrogate in the first place.

If Michelle felt so strongly that I shouldn't be a parent, then why was she our surrogate? I fired off an e-mail. While I was at it, I also asked her what James had meant with his comments about her moving to New York. I'm sure her eyes popped when she opened and read that e-mail.

She ended up apologizing profusely. "I'm so sorry. I would never suggest that both of you would be outside hanging out smoking while your baby was in the house sleeping, crying, or whatever. Even if you guys smoked three packs a day I would still work with you. But, I don't even consider you and David smokers," she wrote. "I mean, my gosh, I think I have seen you with a cigarette in your hand about two times since we've met. I definitely don't judge you and David for anything. I think you are two of the nicest people I have met, and I truly get along so well with you. I'm so sorry. I have a habit of typing or saying the first thing that comes to my mind."

Apology accepted. I don't know that feeling or suffer from that at all myself. So what about James and his comments?

"I do believe that James was joking about it," she wrote. "He is completely supportive of this, please believe that. All in all it really was just a bad joke."

So far, so good. I felt better about the smoking comments and could even understand James joking about Michelle moving to New York. That week had to be very stressful for him and he was probably looking for something to relieve the stress. It was the next part of her e-mail that sent me into a complete and total meltdown.

"You are right in one aspect," she continued. "There was something very wrong while you guys were here and I'm sorry that it boiled over into our time with you and your mom. It's the whole job thing."

Michelle went on to explain how stressful her job had become and how much James wanted her to stay home with the kids. "For a month now," she wrote, "I have been stressing out about the whole thing, coming home from work dog-tired and in no mood to be chatty with my kids. By the end of the work week I was ready to crawl under my bed sheets and stay there." David and I had no idea she was so unhappy.

"The good news," she wrote, "is that I quit my job. Can you believe it?"

No, as a matter of fact, I couldn't believe it. I think my jaw dropped to the floor. How is this possibly good news? Michelle went on to say that she would be babysitting out of their apartment to have some spending money of her own. It was the last thing I expected to hear.

Since day one, David and I really wanted to find someone who was self-sufficient, working a full-time job, as to not be reliant upon any kind of income that resulted from the surrogacy. That had now changed—and it wasn't a welcome change at all. As a matter of fact, it scared the complete hell out of us. What scared me the most was that she was now going to be reliant upon our agency to send her the reimbursement checks. For one thing, none of us were exactly thrilled with the response rate of our agency as it was. Phone calls hadn't been returned, nor had e-mails, and getting anything out of them seemed to be challenging enough—let alone expecting checks to arrive on time.

It also bugged me that she hadn't called or e-mailed to let us know that she was feeling like such a "wreck." Plus, none of her e-mails ever mentioned that there was any kind of friction between her and her husband, let alone that he was expecting her to walk away from a full-time job.

"Quite honestly," Michelle tried to explain, "I didn't want to tell you that I had quit until I had other income. I didn't want you guys to think I was quitting," she wrote, "so I could use surrogacy as a source of income, you know? I know it's something that intended parents worry about, so I just wanted to reassure you."

I admired her for that very much, but David and I started to get an incredible sinking feeling of dread about her decision. It was something that we really wished she had talked to us about before actually doing it. It was also something that we felt so vital to our relationship—to have an income not related to the surrogacy—and now she would be relying on babysitting money as her primary means of income.

Our fears would be justified by the first of the following month. Michelle's check didn't arrive on time. After waiting several days, she sent out an e-mail to the agency. Several nasty e-mails were fired back and forth but nothing seemed to be getting accomplished. Finally, the agency sent us an e-mail to explain their position. "We would be more than happy to wire the money into a checking account for Michelle," the director said, "but she doesn't seem to have one or won't give us the number."

I asked Michelle about it and she said, "No, I don't have a checking account, nor will I get one anytime soon. We don't trust banks. Besides," she continued, "why should I be paying bank fees for balances in an account that I wouldn't have if I wasn't a surrogate for you and David?"

I couldn't figure any of it out. Why wouldn't she have a checking account? It would make life so much easier if the agency could just wire the money directly into her account. But, once again, we were at a standstill. Neither side was willing to budge. I fired off an e-mail to our agency, insisting that they send out a check immediately. It didn't make any difference whether Michelle had a checking account. Our agency promised to be better about getting the checks out on time, yet every month a battle would ensue. David and I could do little on our end, as we had given the agency Michelle's entire fee up front so that it could be put into an escrow account. Then we paid the agency a separate fee to manage that account. So far, they hadn't been managing anything. In the end, Michelle would have to fight that battle on her own. I couldn't help but wonder if she had regretted quitting her job, but didn't dare ask.

It was such a strange feeling knowing that we were daddies in waiting. We were now "IFs," or intended fathers. Pretty much everyone had a positive reaction to the news. At least one or two people honestly thought that we would never get pregnant. One person went as far as proclaiming the conception an "absolute miracle."

I immediately started keeping a scrapbook for our little one: the story of how he or she came to be, letters that his or her birth mother and I exchanged, and some photographs. I especially wanted to keep one letter that Michelle wrote. "Oh my gosh!" she wrote. "This has got to be one of the happiest days of my life. I'm awestruck! Thank you so much for choosing me to help you make a family. These last few months, although they've been stressful, have been so precious to me. I'm just so happy to start our next leg of the journey. I love you guys."

I only wish David's parents were alive to share the excitement. I think they would be very, very proud. David's father had passed away when David was very young. He had lost his mother to breast cancer the year before we met.

Now that the pregnancy was confirmed by the blood test, Michelle called her obstetrician and made an appointment for our very first ultrasound. Once again, because of his schedule, David couldn't get time off from his residency. I would either have to go it alone, or ask Mom if she would go along for the ride again. Of course, she accepted without hesitation.

"I'd love to," she said. "Are you kidding? I wouldn't miss it for the world."

"You just want to know if it's a boy or a girl," I teased her.

"I think it's a girl," she said. "Call it a mother's intuition, but I think it's a girl."

"We'll take anything," I said, "absolutely anything."

Journal Entry, April 2003
I just read an e-mail from Michelle that made my hair stand on end. This whole distance thing is really starting to get to me. I can't go to doctor's appointments or even be there just to offer my help, and it's getting very frustrating. What's wrong with me? Why aren't I on top of the world? We're finding ourselves

*being asked some tough questions and facing more and more
strong opinions all of a sudden. It amazes me how comfortable
people feel to just let us know what they think of what we're doing. I wouldn't dream of questioning someone's right to have a
child of his own, let alone how he was going about doing it.
What do I care? As long as the child is going to be loved and
well taken care of, what difference does it make to me?*

Michelle found a new doctor with privileges at a nearby hospital in
California and went for her eight-week checkup. "Everyone is so nice
and so gay friendly," she wrote, "and when the doctor learned that I
was a surrogate, she was ecstatic!" Other than the fact that she had to
give a lot of blood and endure some poking and prodding, Michelle
said that the appointment went well.

A couple of weeks later it was time for her to go back for another
checkup, mostly to make sure there was a heartbeat. Everything went
well, but little Junior/Miss was in for the ride of his or her life. After
the appointment Michelle sent us an e-mail to let us know that she and
her car had had "a little chat with a guardrail" on the way to the appointment. "It was snowing so badly at the top of one of the hills," she
wrote, "that it was a complete whiteout. I hit a patch of ice, slid across
two lanes of traffic, tapped the guardrail, then slid back over into on-
coming traffic before the car finally stopped. . . . There was no place
to turn around. I had to just keep on going." After telling her to never,
ever do that again, I thanked her for getting our little one accustomed
to having a bumpy ride in life. "It was worth it," Michelle said, "hearing the *whoosh-whoosh* of the heartbeat!"

All along people have been saying things to me such as, "You must
be on top of the world" or, "You probably are walking on air." The
truth is, I'm not anymore. Michelle is starting to show and we're finding ourselves being asked some tough questions and facing more and
more strong opinions.

Michelle and James were the first to come face-to-face with it.
While shopping for maternity clothes, they bumped into an old friend
of theirs. The long-lost friend was just as shocked to see them as they
were to see her shopping for baby clothes. After exchanging hellos
and updates, Michelle offered congratulations on her friend's pregnancy. The incredibly puzzled friend looked at Michelle and then
looked at James and said, "I thought you guys were done having

kids." (They had been friends back when James had undergone a vasectomy.) Not exactly an easy question to answer in the middle of a maternity store!

"We are," James said without missing a beat. "Michelle is a surrogate mother."

"Oh, really?" the quite taken-aback friend asked.

"Yeah," James said. "She's a surrogate for two gay guys in New York!"

If only I could have been a fly on the wall to see the look on that woman's face. A week or so later, Michelle and James found themselves on the telephone with that same friend answering a lot of questions. "At first," Michelle explained, "I thought it was nice of her. Then, the more I thought about it, the angrier I got."

Apparently the friend had given the subject quite a bit of thought and wanted to know why, among other things, James was "letting" Michelle be a surrogate and how she could "just let a child go like that."

"Well," Michelle said, "I couldn't do this without James's support; it's that simple. We're done having children. We have two kids and that's what we've always wanted. It's that simple."

Next, it was my turn. Upon hearing the news that we were officially pregnant, a former—yes, former—friend of ours asked, "Do you really think that this woman is going to give her child to you after all of this?" and then followed up with, "I don't understand how a woman could just give her child away like that."

It was times like those that I honestly didn't know what to say. "Yes," I said, "you're right. The child is Michelle's, and I don't doubt for one second that it's going to be difficult for her. However, it's also my biological child, and Michelle is being reimbursed for carrying it. That's a whopper of a difference."

"Still," my former friend pressed on, "it's almost like she's having the baby to make money, isn't it? I mean, the child is hers and she's being paid to have it, carry it, and hand it over to you."

"The difference is that Michelle set out to do this," I tried to calmly explain. "It's not as if Michelle was already pregnant, before we met, and then asked me if I wanted to buy the baby she was carrying. It's also not as if I approached her after seeing that she was pregnant and asked her if I could buy her unborn child. She set out to do this. We set out to do this. She set out to help someone have a child, but she wasn't pregnant first."

I don't think I ever got through to her. She had made up her mind that what we were doing was wrong, and that was that. What surprised me even more than those conversations were the comments from some of our gay friends. I guess I just automatically assumed that they would all be thrilled for us, but they weren't. Whether they were single or in a relationship, many of them were saying things such as, "Kids? Why would you want them? Are you guys trying to be like straight couples? Why do you want to be a breeder? That's such a straight thing to do. Why don't you just do what we did and get a dog?" The comment that hurt the most was being called a "breeder." I had never heard that term before and, frankly, I hoped that I would never hear it again. It struck me as being so angry, or resentful. So what if I wanted to have a child? That action made me secretly want to be straight? Yeah, I can clearly see the logic there.

It was a strange feeling; it seemed as though David and I were in the minority for even thinking that we should talk about whether we wanted children very early on in our relationship. Talking to other gay couples, such as some of the ones at that holiday party I mentioned before, you could tell very easily when one partner wanted children and the other didn't, as the one who wants children becomes awfully quiet and looks away. The one who wants children is very shy about it, while the one who is dead-set against it makes it perfectly clear that children are not in their future. I imagine it's a real point of contention within a relationship.

To be totally honest, the other issue that was bothering me was money. So far we had invested over $30,000 in having a child of our own, and it's not money that we just had sitting around waiting to be well spent. It's a loan that needs to be repaid. If something should go wrong during the pregnancy or birth—a miscarriage or, God forbid, a stillbirth—that money is completely gone, but the monthly bill will keep right on coming. There simply were no guarantees.

I also remembered being surprised and angry when I first started looking into adoptions and learned that some can run as much as $65,000. Some surrogates were asking as much as $25,000 to $30,000 for reimbursement, and that didn't include agency, legal fees, travel costs, and birth-related medical expenses. The highest I had ever seen was an ad on the very same Web site where Michelle and I met, in which a surrogate was asking for $60,000 in compensation. That's money that most people don't have.

Since when did parenting depend on how much money you had in your bank account? For nontraditional parents like us, the truth is, if we don't have the money, we don't have children. There's something terribly unfair about that. It seems straight people can have as many children as they would like, and my tax dollars go toward raising them. If I, as a gay man, on the other hand, dare to dream of having a child, my partner and I have to pay dearly for it.

So what's the alternative? Adoption is one, which some people seem to prefer, but no guarantees exist with adoption either, and the cost can be just as prohibitive. Plus, in adoptions arranged with mothers-to-be, there's the same risk as in surrogacy, that the birth mother will change her mind at some point during the pregnancy, leaving the adoptive parents, who have invested a great deal of time, effort, and, yes, money, with nothing. At least in surrogacy the birth mother has had a chance to consider her options before she gets pregnant, and there's the comfort of a mutually agreed-upon contract.

David and I were looking fatherhood right in the eyeball, and (to mix metaphors) it was a speeding bullet heading straight at us. We had even started picking out names. We picked both of them after my grandparents on my father's side: Sam for a boy, Lillian for a girl. Of course, we'd call her Lilly. We'll just have to wait and see how camera shy he or she is during the ultrasound.

6

Ultrasound Effects

Journal Entry, May 2003
For half an hour, the earth stood still. All I could see while watching that monitor was my life, my past and future, flashing before my eyes. Maybe it was because we live so far away from Michelle and I haven't seen her since we did the inseminations, but it almost seemed at times as though we weren't actually pregnant. Standing there watching that television monitor brought it all home. What an incredible experience. There's actually someone living in there! Squirming, rolling around, having the time of his or her life.

Our trip to Reno seemed especially grueling this time around. All I could think of on our flight was the upcoming ultrasound, and I couldn't wait to get there. It didn't help matters that sitting across from Mom and me on the airplane was the proud mother of a bouncy and happy eighteen-month-old, blond-haired, blue-eyed little boy. *That's what we're going to have,* I thought to myself. *We're definitely going to have a little boy.*
We landed in Reno and made our way to the "resort" again, and that's when it dawned on me that I hadn't brought Michelle's new cell phone number along, which meant, of course, that I couldn't call her and let her know that we had made it there safely. More important, it also meant I couldn't even find out what time the doctor's appointment was the next day. I had a business card with me on which I had scribbled any and all important phone numbers. However, most, if not all, either didn't have names next to them or had faded beyond recognition thanks to being crammed in my wallet. So, I did the next best thing. I called every number on the business card that even remotely rang a bell as being Michelle's and left message after message. Some unhappy campers were going to come home that night to the following message:

"Hi Michelle, it's me, Mike. Mom and I are here; David sends his love. We're here safe and sound. Hope James and the kids are well. Listen, I can't find your phone number and I don't know what time the doctor's appointment is tomorrow for the ultrasound. I still can't believe we're pregnant, can you? It's the coolest thing. Oh, and does James have to work tomorrow? Okay, well, call when you can; like I said, Mom and I are here. I can't wait to get a peek at that little munchkin in there."

Nice, huh? Mike, Mom, David, Michelle, James, the kids, and the ultrasound. God only knows what people would think.

I was just about driving Mom crazy that night fretting and worrying while I waited for the phone to ring. "Why don't you just get in that huge SUV and drive over there?" she asked. *Good idea,* I thought. Five minutes later we were standing on Michelle's doorstep.

"You're here!" Michelle said in disbelief.

"Yep," I said with a hug, "we made it! Did you get any of the messages I left?" Of course she hadn't. Michelle looked wonderful. She had put on some weight and was starting to show, but seemed to just glow from being pregnant. She was in great spirits.

"Every now and then there's movement," Michelle said as she pointed down to her tummy. "Hopefully she'll move around in there and you can feel it."

I put my hands on Michelle's tummy several times, but wasn't able to feel anything. It was so great to see all of them. James had already left for work, so we stayed for a while, played with the kids a little bit, and then crawled back to the resort to get some shut-eye. Of course, we tried our hand at a couple of slot machines. Mom had become hooked on a slot machine called Texas Tea and couldn't resist the temptation. I couldn't either. They were nickel slots, after all. The problem was that you had to lug twenty dollars of nickels around in a plastic cup all night.

The next day we met up with Michelle again after stopping by the drug store to buy a VHS tape for the ultrasound, then we headed off on the half-hour drive to California for the doctor's appointment.

Before we knew it, Michelle was lying down on the exam table having jelly spread all over her bulging belly. Within seconds, a tiny black and white life-form appeared on the overhead monitor. It was truly incredible. Fuzzy, blurry white images started to become crystal clear against the stark black monitor. There "it" was, happy as a clam and not a care in the world.

"Don't even think of starting to cry, Michael," Michelle said, "or I'm going to start crying."

"Too late," I said. "You're too late."

The three of us watched as the black television monitor lit up with signs of squiggling, squirming, and thumb sucking. All of it was amazingly clear but somehow so unreal. The very first image that came on the screen was of the baby sucking his or her thumb.

The ultrasound technician checked to make sure all was okay and even pointed out the stomach, kidneys, spine, and heart. However, she seemed to be having trouble figuring out the gender.

"If you'd like," she turned to us and said, "you can go outside, walk around, even jump around—just go and move around a little bit, then come back in and we'll try to see whether it's a him or a her."

You never saw three people move faster in your life. Half an hour later we were back. Michelle was covered with jelly again, and after what seemed like an eternity and some heavy poking and prodding, the tech turned to us and asked, "You do want to know the gender, right?"

All three of us said, "Yes!" in unison.

"Well," she said, "I'm ninety-five percent certain that you're going to be having a little girl. She's got her legs crossed pretty tightly," she continued, "so I can't be one hundred percent certain. But I'd bet you it's a girl."

Good, I thought, *let's hope she keeps them like that until she's at least thirty*—I'm certainly not going to be ready to be called Grandpa anytime soon.

For the next half an hour, the earth just simply stood still. All I could see while watching that monitor was my life, my past and future flashing before my eyes.

While I watched our baby girl on the monitor, I remembered coming out to my mother and how she hung her head and cried. The last thing a son wants to do is make his own mother cry, but that's all she could do. I remembered her saying, "You won't be able to have children of your own, Michael, and you would be such a wonderful father."

I reminded her that there would probably be options open to us by then.

"True," Mom said, "that's true. But it's a long and difficult road from now until then, and you never know. It's such a shame." Now, almost seventeen years later, there we were watching my daughter having the time of her life. I looked over at Mom and thought about how far we had come; she caught my gaze and broke down in tears.

I also kept looking over at Michelle. Her eyes were glued to the monitor and all she could do was smile and giggle. I thought about how remarkable it was to be standing in a room with my mother and my surrogate mother watching my very own daughter right before my eyes.

Then I flashed to the future and saw our little girl running around the yard laughing and giggling without a care in the world. It's the kind of giggle that goes right to your heart and pierces your soul.

> *Journal Entry, May 2003*
> *Having Mom at the ultrasound was just the most amazing experience. I'm so thrilled she came with me. I still can't believe she was there. I don't know who's happier that we're pregnant: me, David, or my mother. Standing there with her today watching that tiny little life-form squirming around was just an incredible feeling. I'm very lucky. No, I'm incredibly lucky.*

On the way back to Nevada, I actually turned around to look at Michelle and asked, "So, will we do this again when David is ready?" She was as surprised by my question as I was. I think my mother almost passed out.

"Wow," Michelle said, "I can't believe you would even want or think of doing this again with me!"

I asked her why.

"It hasn't been easy all the time, you know," she said with her eyebrows furrowed, "but I'm so honored that you would ask me again. I don't know. I would do it. I don't know if James would be for going through all of this again." We all sat silently as we made our way into town and then Michelle burst out in laughter. "Mike's going to be a daddy! Mike's going to be a daddy!" she repeated.

"How cool is that?" I asked. "How cool is that?" I looked over at Mom and she was still in tears.

Our friends back home had a field day with the thought of my having a daughter. I've made my fair share of wisecracks to David about being a gynecologist and choosing to closely examine parts of a woman's body that I've never even seen. "God has a sense a humor, doesn't he?" asked one of our friends. "Now you're going to have to see a vulva close-up for a few years."

"Yes," I said. "She does have a wonderful sense of humor."

Once we got back home, Michelle and our agency almost came to blows over her monthly reimbursement and compensation checks. David and I spent a weekend reading some pretty nasty e-mails that were being sent back and forth between them. All we could do was sit back and watch. There was even talk of a breach of contract and legal intervention. I could tell that Michelle wanted us to do something. I just wasn't sure what we could do other than call them, which of course we did, but all we heard was the answering machine. So, I did the next best thing and fired off an e-mail demanding that they get the check out to Michelle. Thankfully, it seemed to have resolved itself, as it had in the past, with repeated promises by the agency to get the checks out on time.

Just for reassurance, I picked up the phone and called an attorney with whom I had spoken when we were trying to figure out if surrogacy was legal in New York. She reminded me that compensation is a touchy subject. She said, "If it's in your contract that she gets her check on the first of the month then she does have legal recourse. The problem is, if either you, or your surrogate, file a lawsuit against your agency, she just might not get the remainder of her fee, as they could simply shut their doors." Leave it to an attorney to point out additional complications.

"I don't know if I want to go through all of this when it's my turn," David said. Once again, I honestly didn't know what to say. I felt terribly guilty, as we had agreed that I would go first mainly because of my employer offering day care, which wasn't being offered anymore. Now, to hear him so discouraged, I started wishing that he had gone first.

"I don't know how you're doing all of this, Michael," David said to me with his head down. "It's been so much stress. I don't know if I could do it when it's my turn. Maybe we should look into adoption when we're ready to do it again?" I didn't know how to answer him. I just felt terrible.

"It has been hard, I know. It's almost as though we're married to Michelle and James, isn't it?" I asked. "Whatever they do, whatever decision that they make directly affects us, and it's just a feeling that I can't get used to. But keep in mind, this is our first time around and we're learning a lot, aren't we?" I asked.

"Yes," David said, "we certainly are. If anything, we're learning what *not* to do."

That night we popped the tape of the ultrasound into the VCR and reminded ourselves what was most important: we were going to be daddies.

Our next step was signing all of the paperwork for a prebirth order, which, along with our contract, would have to go before a judge in California. Once signed and reviewed, it would be court-ordered that the birth certificate be altered to reflect David as "mother." Our names would both be on the legal birth certificate. That was just one of the perks of delivering in the state of California, the only state that allows such a thing to happen.

Journal Entry, May 2003
Seeing the ultrasound was a truly amazing experience—it made everything so real. It's not a dream anymore. It's real. It's really happening. We're finally pregnant. But I came home with a strange feeling. One part of me is excited and thrilled, the other part can't wait for this all to be over. I'm tired of surprises and bombshells. I'm tired of worrying about finances and sudden changes to everything. It's becoming too much to handle all on my own. Michelle is looking out for herself a lot and rightfully so. I just can't shake this feeling of not being able to wait until it's all finally over with.

Our official due date was October 11, 2003. David and I started to make arrangements to be there in person for the delivery. However, a week or so later, Michelle e-mailed to let us know that at her most recent doctor's appointment, the due date had changed to October 5. When I told David about it, I knew there was going to be a problem.

"I think one of the other residents has already asked for that week off," David said with a look of shock and disgust. "I put in for the week of the eleventh a month ago. I don't know if I can change it now." That meant that there was a very good chance that he wasn't going to be able to see his own daughter being born. I sent an e-mail out to Michelle.

"How do you feel about being induced?" I asked. "It doesn't look as though David is going to be able to make the new date, as he's already asked and gotten approval for time off on the eleventh. So, we're thinking of having an induction done and need to know how you feel about it. We're also thinking about having it done on October 1. Just let us know what you think." I didn't expect Michelle's response at all.

"First of all," she wrote, "I think it's a four-letter word! I was induced with my son and it sucked a big one!" She added, "I would prefer not to be induced at all, but am totally willing to do it if it means having both of you there for the delivery."

"That's good," I wrote back, "because I remember you said that James didn't want any part of being there, understandably, so if we waited until the day you went into delivery you might just be doing a lot of pushing and shoving alone."

> *Journal Entry, May 2003*
> *Michelle has been doing a lot of complaining about money lately. First it was the compensation checks, now it's that her maternity allowance check is late. I keep wondering if it would be different if she had kept her job. I know that's probably not right, but I keep thinking about it. She's also been talking a lot about how they've been spending the compensation money and I am feeling strange about that. They're buying this and that and planning a trip to Disneyland. I wish I felt happy that she is bringing in enough money to buy nice things and take nice trips with her family, so why aren't I? What kind of a person isn't happy for someone else?*

Have you ever felt a certain way about something and been surprised by how you felt? I started feeling resentful. Yes, resentful. Michelle had been innocently mentioning what she had been buying and how they had been spending the money from her compensation checks and I was resenting every minute of it. I couldn't believe how I was feeling. I even tried to deny it. I tried ignoring my feelings. I didn't want to admit that I was that type of person. However, I didn't like hearing about it at all. I think it had something to do with the fact that it was talking about money and a baby, period. *Spend the money any way you want,* I thought, *but don't tell me how you're spending it.* I didn't want or need to know. I also felt myself judging how the money was being spent, if you can believe that.

"They aren't using the money as a down payment on a house, or investing it," I said to David. "They are just spending it on everything and anything."

"Good for them," David said with a look of surprise.

"But it's our money they're spending," I said, not believing I had even said it.

"It's their money," David said firmly. "They can spend it on anything they want. Sure, it would be nice if they were saving it for a down payment on a house, but they can spend it any way they want."

"It's really none of my business, I know," I said in defeat.

It was the money thing again. I had been going back to the Web site that both Michelle and I subscribed to and a lot of the surrogates wrote that most intended parents worry about one thing and one thing only: money. I can honestly say it's true. Money is a huge issue. I was reminded of our very first conversation with the agency months ago, when I said that I didn't want our arrangement to be a matter of the "haves" and the "have-nots." What I did think was wonderful was that Michelle wasn't spending money on herself. She was spending it on her family, just as she had said that she would when we were first getting to know each other. It was obvious that she felt grateful that they were going through this journey right along with her. I think it was her way of thanking them for being so supportive of her.

Journal Entry, June 2003
Michelle e-mailed last night and said that the baby's heartbeat was very strong at 140 beats per minute. Her tummy is measuring a little bit ahead, too. Then she said that the doctor told her she was happy that it wasn't her that was going to be pushing this baby out! I was a little concerned though, as she keeps mentioning how much weight she's either gained or hasn't gained. She didn't want her weight to be an issue, but it seems like she's worried about gaining any weight at all. I can't figure that out. We're not making her weight an issue and never have, but she sure seems to be.

It had been a tough couple of weeks, but all I had to do was keep popping that tape of the ultrasound into the VCR and keep reminding myself why we were doing all of this, and that it was all worth it. The fact of the matter was if I thought the past few weeks had been rough, the next few weeks would be even worse—they would prove to be the most trying and stressful weeks of our entire journey.

–7–

Last-Minute Complications

Journal Entry, August 2003
*Well, we were just hit with another bombshell. It was the last
thing that we needed. If it wasn't bad enough waiting to find out
about this insurance, now Michelle e-mails and tells us that they
are moving to another state! They're moving to Arizona by the
end of the month! Now what? I'm not even sure if surrogacy is
legal in Arizona, and it sounds like she's several hours away
from California. I'm so angry and hurt and confused right now
I'm beside myself. This whole thing could get ugly, and I mean
really ugly. Can we stop her from moving? Should we stop her?
What are we going to do about a doctor? What about where
she's going to deliver? She doesn't have health insurance. I
have so many phone calls to make it's not funny. But I honestly
don't even know where to begin.*

With our new due date of October 1 getting closer by the moment,
we were trying to just keep ourselves very busy and get everything in
place for the big day. We were also trying to figure out whether
James's insurance company was even going to cover the pregnancy,
labor, and delivery. Michelle had sent us an e-mail that sent us reeling. Neither she, nor James, was sure that his insurance was going to
cover labor and delivery because it's a surrogacy arrangement. I set
out to try and find some answers. However, after many phone calls to
insurance companies and even hiring someone to help us find insurance for Michelle, we finally learned that we were searching for the
impossible. No insurance company was going to take on what they
called "a preexisting condition," especially not a full-blown pregnancy. That meant that all expenses, from the remaining prenatal care
to labor and delivery, would now have to be paid out-of-pocket. It
wasn't a complete surprise, as the more phone calls I made the less

likely it appeared that it would work out otherwise. I was furious and very scared, but the fact of the matter was that we should have taken care of it months ago when there were clear red flags that something was terribly wrong, or that at least something could go terribly wrong. We hadn't prepared, nor had we taken the signs seriously. We were now going to pay dearly for our decisions.

"I'm so sorry that I sprang the insurance on you," Michelle wrote shortly after our trip out for the ultrasound. "I just kept waiting for a time to talk to you privately about it while you were here, and then our whole trip went by. I know it's a huge bombshell. Believe me, it is for us, too. I'm just so sorry," she continued. "If I had any idea that the insurance was going to change, I sure wouldn't have quit my job. But, how could we have known, you know?"

I contacted our long-lost agency to get their advice, only to learn that Michelle had e-mailed them as well. The agency director e-mailed me to let us know that they were going to call the insurance company directly and hopefully get to the bottom of whether they would cover the pregnancy. Surprisingly, Michelle warned against it. "If you do call, I wouldn't mention names," she wrote in an e-mail that the agency then forwarded to us. "I'm not even sure if we're covered anymore (by insurance) and that's a headache that I would rather not worry about unless you can find a way to put it all on Mike and David. Sorry. I guess I'm just really tired."

Reading that e-mail certainly didn't make us feel any better, but then again, it wasn't meant to. It was a matter of Michelle basically saying that this wasn't her problem—it's theirs. It was our problem, our big problem.

The trouble was, it wasn't the only problem we were being faced with. To try and at least put our minds at ease, I immediately started calling hospitals on the West Coast in a feeble attempt to try and get an estimate of how much we would end up paying. Prices ranged anywhere between $4,000 and $6,000 for labor and delivery alone. All other fees would be paid separately, including the obstetrician and anesthesiologist. The total bill looked as though it could come close to $10,000.

In the meantime, it was on to our next issue: our prebirth order. In mid-July we found an attorney in California who would draw up the paperwork to have both of our names, David's and mine, appear on the birth certificate. It's a process that takes about a month to complete, including having a judge in California sign off on the paperwork and make it official. Everything seemed to be going along a little more smoothly, and we could finally take a breather and do some anticipated baby shopping. A stroller, Pack 'n Play, and several outfits later, we were hit with yet another bombshell.

Michelle had learned from a private insurance sales rep that hospitals, particularly in California, offer a discount if you are paying out-of-pocket for all expenses.

"The hospital the insurance rep is talking about," Michelle wrote, "is actually in San Diego. Whoa, you say, that's really far away!" she continued. "But not as far as you think! Remember me telling you before that James had been chewing on the idea of moving back to Arizona? Well, we've finally made the decision that we will be moving there."

I simply couldn't believe what I had just read. I know I've said that before, but this one was a true-blue jaw-dropper of an e-mail. What made it worse was the fact that it was put so nonchalantly. I was stunned. Suddenly we went from finding out that we didn't have health insurance to cover our baby or our surrogate, but now we're finding out that she's moving to another state. Oh, it gets better.

Michelle would not only be moving several hours away from the nearest city in California, but I wasn't even sure if surrogacy was legal in Arizona. The last I knew, surrogacy, whether paid or unpaid, was in fact illegal, but as of 1994 that ruling was still being battled out in the courts. What if Michelle started having complications and had to deliver in Arizona rather than California? What would that mean for our prebirth order? Could we come home with our baby? What about the birth certificate? Would I have to adopt? Would David? My head was spinning with questions.

"Is she trying to drive me insane?" I asked a bewildered, dazed, and confused David. "I'm actually afraid to open any more of her e-mails," I said, "because every time I do I think I'm going to die from a heart attack."

Okay, so that was a little dramatic. However, if I hadn't been grinding my teeth and suffering from a twitching eyelid before, my eyeball could have popped right out of its socket and rolled around New York City with that revelation.

Oddly enough, Michelle's e-mail was enthusiastic. "You guys could fly right into San Diego," she wrote, "which would mean a much shorter trip."

"Well woohoo!" I said to David. "Let's get our travel agent on the phone! Oh, forget that, that would be me. I'm our travel agent." David was far from amused.

I didn't know where to even begin having a meltdown, or over what issue specifically. Let's see, no health insurance, which is going to cost us thousands of dollars, and now moving to another state. Is there anything else? We're now delivering in San Diego, which is six hours away by car, instead of a forty-five-minute drive that it had been. What else? Well, we don't have a hospital to deliver in, nor do we have an obstetrician. If I told you that we were completely stressed out and totally aggravated, it would be the understatement of the century. I was in such a panic that I literally froze—until David came home that night, that is.

"This can't be happening," I said to David. "This just cannot be happening. Everything we've planned has now completely fallen apart. When will this nightmare end?"

If there was any saving grace, it was that Michelle seemed willing to compromise with us. "I could go to San Diego early," she wrote, "and at worst I would be out there for three weeks without James and the kids. I mean I didn't get into surrogacy thinking there would be no sacrifice, and I sure didn't think that it would all be sunshine and rainbows!" Sunshine and rainbows it was not.

"Or," she continued, "if you have to get a separate insurance policy for this pregnancy I could stay right here, and James and the kids would move to Arizona." At least we had options, or so I thought.

Our first thought was that there was no way that we could let Michelle pack up and move to Arizona being eight months pregnant with our child. It was way too risky. I put a call in to the same attorney who had been helping us with our prebirth order. "I wouldn't let her move," our attorney said. "She's doing something so wonderful for you, yes, that's a given, but there comes a time when you just have to put your foot down and say no, you're not moving." It was easy for her to say.

Our heads were spinning with questions. If we did sue we would have to go to court. Did we honestly want things to get that ugly? Would we win our case if we did? The only way to answer that question was to have our attorney take a look at the contract. Sure enough, there was little that we could do. If James and Michelle were packing up and moving out of state we had no choice but to accept the news and roll with the punches because our contract didn't including inhib-iting travel after a certain number of weeks into a pregnancy, let alone to another state. I had heard of other intended parents adding such a clause in their contracts but couldn't for the life of me figure out why they would stipulate something like that. Now I knew.

"You might have a huge problem on your hands," our attorney said in yet another phone call. "As far as I can see a surrogacy agreement or contract might be illegal in the state of Arizona. What if Michelle has complications," she asked, "and the child has to be delivered there?" "Good question," I said. Very, very good question. If the child was born in Arizona it could be very difficult to have my name added to the birth certificate, and I'm the biological father. It would also prove to be nearly impossible to have David's name added at all. To do that, David would need to apply for a stepparent adoption, which is not only time-consuming, but invasive and costly. All of a sudden, with only eight weeks to go, our surrogacy journey was taking a huge left turn—out of nowhere.

At first, I was furious. I felt helpless and completely trapped. Then, the self-loathing settled in. I blamed myself for not taking care of the insurance issue when it reared its ugly head. I also blamed myself for not having the guts to fight for what we felt was right—to have Michelle stay in Nevada and deliver in South Lake Tahoe as we had agreed. I have been in very few situations in my life where I have felt so completely overwhelmed with anger—not having a choice in a matter is one of them. This was the stuff that my worst nightmares were made of. The problem was, who to direct my anger toward? For days I walked around furious and beside myself. It took several days and long, long, talks with friends, family, and David before I could settle down and even begin to sort things through. We had an attorney waiting for a yes or no as to whether we would sue Michelle to try and block her from moving, an agency that was useless, and thousands of dollars in medical bills looming in the near future. More important, we had a child. A child who had no idea what was going on, a child that didn't ask to be brought into this mess—especially a court battle—a child who was completely innocent. I woke up one night in a cold sweat and wrote in my diary.

Journal Entry, August 2003
Part of me wants to go after Michelle and James with both bar-rels loaded and slap them with a flat-out law suit. How dare they

do this? Why can't this wait? Why do they have to move now of all times? Why now? Don't they realize what this is doing to us? How am I going to find Michelle an obstetrician? How will I ever find her a hospital? How are we going to afford to fly her back and forth to San Diego five or six times between now and when she delivers? How can we afford to pay for her meals, her hotels, and her transportation on top of paying all the expenses related to labor and delivery? Why are they doing this? I have to know why. Every cell in my body is angry. I am furious down to my very soul. I feel like my stomach, heart, and soul are on fire with rage. But it's useless. My rage isn't changing anything. No one wants to hear about my rage. Our child certainly doesn't. I don't want to bring a child into this world if it's going to be filled with anger, resentment, and hostility. She doesn't deserve it. I won't have it. Not my child. I simply won't have it.

It took days for me to realize that my anger was useless and that it wasn't going to help; it would only hinder the progress that we had to make. We have a baby on the way and dozens of decisions to make. There simply wasn't time for anger, but I was still furious.

One day on my lunch break I headed over to the bookstore to find something, anything, about anger and anger management. I stumbled upon a book in the self-help section that involved tapping yourself: *Getting thru to Your Emotions with EFT: Tap into Your Hidden Potential with the Emotional Freedom Techniques* by Phillip and Jan Mountrose. *Okay,* I thought, *I'll give it a try as long as no one, and I mean no one, sees me doing it.* It actually seemed to work, or at least offered relief. I would lie in bed while David was snoring away and focus on an emotion—could it be anger? Then, while concentrating and repeating a phrase, I would tap certain pressure points on my face and neck. After poking myself in the eye—more like jabbing myself in the eye, with so much pent-up anger coming out—I did gradually feel relief. Believe me, no one was a bigger critic than me—but I had to calm down and focus.

I could now address some of the issues. The first obstacle was finding a hospital that would accept cash as a payment for an uninsured mother. Next I had to find a new obstetrician. On top of that, I had to figure out a way to get Michelle from Arizona to San Diego for prenatal appointments and the actual delivery. I started making dozens of phone calls from work and from home. "How's it going, Twitch?" a co-worker asked as she was passing by my desk. All I could do was growl.

"So let me get this straight," a receptionist at an obstetrics office said while trying to understand everything that I had just spewed forth. "You are a gay couple living in New York and you have a surrogate mother who lives in Nevada, but who is moving to Arizona and wants to deliver in California."

All I could muster was, "Uh-huh."

"And she's eight months pregnant. She has no health insurance and you are agreeing to pay for all services out-of-pocket. Correct?"

"Uh, uh-huh," I mumbled.

"She's had prenatal care, but doesn't have a doctor here, right?"

"Uh-huh," I repeated.

"So, now you need to find an obstetrician willing to take on an existing pregnancy and deliver the child at an undetermined hospital. How am I doing so far?"

I couldn't even answer. I was speechless. Finally, I managed to say that I would call her right back, but not before my voice cracked and went up twenty-five octaves. I immediately got up from my desk and raced across the room, making a beeline for the bathroom.

"Are you okay, Twitch?" someone asked as I raced by. All I could say was an expletive. Sorry, but there was no time for witty repartee. I needed to get somewhere, fast. I sat down on the toilet and immediately started tapping. "This stress . . . this stress," I said repeatedly. I'm sure my co-workers could have heard me drilling away on my forehead if they listened closely enough. "This fear . . . this fear," I said, still drilling, I mean tapping, away. I stopped tapping and the emotions starting pouring out. I had myself a good cry and then went right back to my desk and actually picked up the phone.

"Yes," I said to the receptionist who couldn't believe I actually did call her back, "everything you said before? It's all true and that just about sums it up."

"I hope you don't mind my saying this, Mike," she said with a sigh and slight disbelief, "but this is the biggest mess I've ever heard of and I've been working at this office for almost fifteen years. You are trying to do the impossible. I'm sorry, Mike. It's just impossible."

I actually tried tapping my way through that entire statement but didn't make it far before I was in tears. "I just need someone to help me," I said, now completely hysterical. "Why can't someone just help me? I didn't ask for this." I had totally lost it. "I didn't do anything wrong. I'm trying. I'm honestly trying to do everything that I can do and I'm sitting here at work tapping myself on the forehead and crying and I can't do it anymore."

Do you think she regretted ever answering that phone call or what? This was the stuff that you go home and tell your husband, "You won't believe the phone call I had today—not once—but twice!"

I had called two or three hospitals in the San Diego area and spoken with countless people. I had also called nearly a dozen private obstetricians seeking help. However, this was the first time someone was honest about what we were trying to do. After listening to me sob and babble on about surrogates and tapping myself she agreed to at least ask around the office. I was desperate, and she knew it. Either that or she was afraid that if she didn't help me I'd call back a third time.

"I'm not making any promises," she said before hanging up. "I am truly sorry this is happening. I'll do my absolute best to help you out."

I never, ever, thought that I would hear from that woman again. To this day I swear she was an angel sent by God. I just hoped it wasn't COD, because we were going to need every penny we had.

I was still trying to figure out how much all of this was going to cost us. If we were lucky enough to find an obstetrician for Michelle, they were going to want to see her before delivery at least several times, as she was eight months along. Plus, we would have to fly Michelle out there, put her up in a hotel, pay for a rental car, and provide for meals and entertainment for at least two weeks prior to the due date. The dollar signs were quickly adding up.

I e-mailed Michelle with our final decision. "Unfortunately," I wrote, "we're going to have to insist that you stay behind in Nevada. It's not something that's easy to ask, but we think it's only fair." Days went by before I heard anything back from her. My gut told me she had read the e-mail and didn't like it.

The very next morning I was driving a colleague to a photo shoot when she made the huge mistake of asking me how things were going with the baby. I went off on a half-hour tirade and had all I could do to stop myself from tapping my nose off while in the car.

"Mike, the answer is simple," she blurted out. "Michelle can move wherever the hell she wants to—let her move to Timbuktu if that's

what turns her on—what matters is that she damn well better get back
to Tahoe, where her doctor and hospital are."

I couldn't believe my ears. She was right.

"I mean," she went on, "her doctor is there, the hospital is there,
and the staff knows of your situation, and it's still in California."

Finally, I had a moment of clarity. With that, we called Michelle
that weekend and told her that we had changed our minds.

"That's good," she said, much to our surprise, "because I didn't
know how I was going to tell you no, I wasn't going to stay behind."
The bottom line was that Michelle was moving to Arizona whether
anyone liked it or not. "James has a new job there," she would later
write. "We have to take care of our family first." Michelle preregis-
tered at the hospital in Tahoe two weeks later.

Deciding that she would move to Arizona but return to Tahoe for
labor and delivery was great, but we still didn't know how it was all
going to work out. Eventually we decided to fly her back to Tahoe and
put her up in a hotel one week before the due date of October 1.

"So, who's paying for all of this?" I asked Michelle in an e-mail.

"I would think that you and David would pay for my transportation, airfare, hotel, and entertainment," she quickly replied.

Her justification was that if she had stayed behind in Nevada rather
than move with her family to Arizona she would have to pay rent and
that wasn't fair. I didn't quite understand that rationale, but honestly, I
just wanted everything to be over. I had simply had enough. Whatever
we had to pay we would pay. Michelle did offer to pay for her entertainment, although I wasn't sure what a nine-month pregnant woman
does for entertainment. I don't *want* to know.

"We need something to celebrate," my slightly overwhelmed-by-
all-the-bad-news mother said. "This is supposed to be a happy and
exciting time for you guys, and instead you're a stressed-out mess.
We need to have a baby shower," she said. "We have to celebrate this."

That news hit me like a ton of bricks. All I could think of was that it
was another thing to plan and schedule and coordinate.

"Your sister and I will take care of everything," Mom said. "Don't
worry about anything."

Funny, I thought, *someone else said that to me, oh, about nine
months ago and look where that got us.* Three weeks later we found
ourselves sitting under a huge white tent, wearing the traditional, yet
incredibly embarrassing, bow-hat made from paper plates covered

with bows taken from all of our gifts, surrounded by family and close friends, doing a little celebrating. Mom's champagne-with-some-extra-booze-thrown-in-for-good-measure punch was the biggest hit of the day!

I have to admit that it felt very strange to sit next to David in the midst of a baby shower; I mean, two men having a baby surrounded by family and friends. Who would ever have thought?

"Isn't this something?" David asked.

"Yep," I said, "it really is."

What seemed even stranger was the amount of pink clothes people bought as gifts!

Two weeks later we were invited to a birthday party for one of David's co-workers. He had grown close to the nurses on the floor where he worked and we welcomed the invitation to relax and have some fun. Little did we know it was actually a surprise baby shower thrown for the two nervous dads to be! There were more funny bow-hats and more adorable pink outfits. We couldn't believe the generosity of people and how supportive they were being. A room filled with at least twenty women, all gathered together to welcome us into the world of parenting. It was truly amazing. A few days later we found ourselves folding four loads of laundry on a Sunday afternoon. I had to make a last-minute phone call to Mom just to make sure I shouldn't add fabric softener to the mix as we were washing baby clothes. With blankets, clothes, cloth diapers, and towels all around us we turned to each other and both started to cry. Another bit of good news was that our prebirth order had appeared before a judge in Los Angeles County and had been officially signed, sealed, and certified. I had jotted an e-mail to Michelle the week before letting her know that our attorney had called and said that it was sitting in front of a judge and would be signed within days. When the good news came I went online to share it with some friends. Little did I know something so innocent would wind up causing so many problems!

Journal Entry, September 2003
So, I just got a really nasty e-mail from Michelle telling me that she thought it was "pretty crappy" that I didn't let her know about the prebirth order first. Then she went on to say that she had many other issues with us that she wanted to go into but thought she shouldn't. She has issues? I've nearly tapped my face off, have no front teeth left, and she has issues? We're flying

her here and there, putting her up in a hotel, have agreed to pay all expenses that have ever been thrown at us, you name it, and she's got issues? Honey, you don't know issues. Give me a break already.

Just when I thought it was safe to open an e-mail, I had one waiting for me in my inbox from Michelle. "I think it's pretty crappy," her e-mail began, "that you didn't let me know first that the prebirth order was done. That is a very important piece of paper and you didn't feel it justified a quick e-mail to me. I think that says a lot about where this journey has gone in the last few months." She was angry, very angry, and it was about time that we all cleared the air. "I know you can't be happy with the way this whole relationship has turned," she concluded. "I know I'm not." She was right again. We were far from happy with how the relationship had been going the past few months. Tap. Tap. Tap!

Journal Entry, September 2003
I woke up this morning with a splitting headache and my face hurts. My face hurts? Well, I think I did so much tapping that I tapped myself out of anger but into pain. Who comes up with these self-help remedies, anyway? Now I have to find out if I can tap myself out of pain.

While I thought about how I was going to respond to Michelle's e-mail, it was time to put my part-time travel agent hat on again. This time canceling the reservations I had made in San Diego, including doctor's appointments, and making new reservations for Tahoe. Believe it or not, the receptionist that I had spoken with weeks before—you know, the one who bore the brunt of my sobbing—had in fact called back and said, "As a courtesy to your partner, David (being a fellow doctor), one of the obstetricians here on staff has agreed to work with you and your surrogate mother. She'll need to come out here twice a week for the remainder of her pregnancy, though, so we're not sure how we're going to make it work, but let us know."

Thankfully, we didn't have to worry about it. I called the office again, though, just to let her know how much we appreciated her efforts.

It took a few days, but I finally responded to Michelle's e-mail and let her know that I was not the least bit happy about the e-mail she had sent. It wasn't an easy thing to do. In fact, it took a lot of thought and soul-searching, not to mention tapping. See, all along we had it in the back of our minds that we would work with Michelle again so that our children would at least have a biological connection through their birth mom. We wanted our child to have a sibling so that she could have someone to pal around with and also another means of love and support. The problem was that it kept me from being totally honest and saying things that I normally would have said. If Michelle became angry with us, and we became angry with her, chances were that we wouldn't end up working with each other again. However, her e-mail changed that. I also knew that she was just as furious with us over their move to Arizona as we were with them. I sensed all along that Michelle felt that we were making a big deal out of nothing, and we felt they were making light of a big deal.

"I did e-mail you and let you know that the prebirth order was in fact in front of a judge and ready to be signed. You never responded to that e-mail," I wrote. "You also let us know that you weren't going to be checking e-mails all that often after your move to Arizona, so why would I waste time in waiting to hear back from you when I had no idea when you would be checking messages? I have every right to share whatever news I care to with anyone and I certainly don't need your permission to do so."

"I think what you are sensing," I continued, "is that our friendship has been strained. On our end, we haven't felt that our feelings or needs have been considered in many of the decisions that you and James have made. It's been a feeling of, well, just go along for the ride, as there's not much we can do except go along with it." I was far from over. "David and I have done our absolute best to treat you well and take care of our end of things. We've had a lot of bombshells dropped on us and have done nothing more than rolled with a lot of punches, and we've handled them with patience and understanding. We've treated you very, very well from day one, so I don't have any idea what you feel that we have done that you would need to vent about. Be honest with us," I concluded, "and clear the air. I don't want my child to be born under false pretenses."

It didn't take long for Michelle to fire back.

"I do apologize for not getting back to the e-mail where you said the prebirth order was in front of the judge. I could have sworn that I had replied, but looking back at my log, I realized I didn't. I'm truly sorry. Overall," she continued, "you have been really good about han-dling everything that has been thrown at you as far as insurance. I guess my biggest pet peeve with this whole thing, though, is your nonhandling of the agency issue. It irked us that you were so blasé about the medical bills. I understand that you had given them the money to pay the bills," she continued, "but when they failed to do it, you just seemed like you were twiddling your thumbs, saying 'it's not our problem' when it WAS your problem." (For the record, I was not twiddling, I was twitching.) "The way I've been feeling is they aren't even willing to go to bat with the agency on something, yet they expect me to still be happy and nice and everything?"

As far as David and I feeling that we weren't considered in their decisions, Michelle would explain that she felt a little "miffed" that we would think that we needed to be consulted about it. "I understand your apprehension about me giving birth outside of California, I re-ally do," Michelle wrote. "However, I just feel you might be the same way had we moved to somewhere else in Nevada that was farther than I am now. We had to make a decision for our family. It wasn't conve-nient, but life isn't very convenient, know what I mean?"

I was so angry after reading her e-mail that I could have tapped my face off, then gone and tapped David's face off.

Weeks before, Michelle had said that she was receiving past-due notices and threatening letters from bill collectors regarding out-standing bills related to her prenatal care. Those bills totaled a little over $400. She had apparently sent the receipts and bills to our lovely agency that, in turn, never paid them. Through a series of phone calls and e-mails, our agency claimed that they had never received any of the bills, or they would have paid them promptly. Did I believe them? Not for a second.

"Please, just send us the unpaid bills," I wrote in an e-mail to Michelle. "We'll gladly pay them. I don't want your credit history ru-ined over a couple of hundred dollars. It's stupid and not worth it."

Sadly, Michelle never did send us the bills. We couldn't pay bills that we didn't have. I couldn't and still don't understand how or why David and I shouldn't have been included on major decisions such as quitting a job or moving out of state. How could it not affect us? It had a direct effect upon us—our emotions and our pocketbooks.

Something else hit me—like a lead balloon—while I was trying to put myself in Michelle's shoes and understand how she was feeling and why she was so angry. "It could be just hormones," a friend of ours said. "She's probably a hormonal mess, being almost nine months pregnant. She'll say anything and act any way she damn well pleases. She's a mess."

"*She's* a mess," I said. "Please! Look at me! This is a mess!"

We had been on one hell of a roller-coaster ride the past few weeks, but our due date was just weeks away. We had a lot of shopping and getting ready to bring a baby home. We were going to be daddies very, very soon, and that's all that really mattered.

8

It's a Girl!

Journal Entry, October 2003
It's now two o'clock in the morning. Mom and Dad are here.
This house is way too small. We're trying not to trip over one
another. What are we going to do when the baby comes? I need a
bigger house. No, what I need is to sleep. I've been lying in bed
twitching and tapping. I wish I could tap myself into a coma, or
at least to sleep for a couple hours! We leave for California in
two hours and I'm wide awake. David is sick and is already
dropping hints that he might not be able to fly in the morning.
What? Is this for real? He's going to miss the delivery of his
daughter? It's unbelievable. I wonder how Michelle is doing.

The alarm clock went off at four-thirty in the morning, but I was already wide awake. Today was the day. The day we had been waiting for. In just a few short hours I was going to become a father. With everything that had been going on in the past few months I started feeling as though I was in the middle of a whirlwind. There wasn't time to be scared. No time for doubts. I was going to be a father in a few short hours, but first, I had to make it all the way across the country with my sick-as-a-dog partner and my mother. David had spent the entire night throwing up after eating ketchup that had been in the refrigerator since we bought our house three years ago. So much for my thinking condiments never spoil. He woke up feeling a little bit better than he had the night before, but still wasn't sure if he was well enough to fly. I was beyond bitchy. I'm not at my best at certain times of the day and four-thirty in the morning, I learned, was definitely one of them. Mom was downstairs making a cup of coffee and asked if I was able to get any sleep.

"No," I said, still half in a stupor.

"It's a lot to have on your mind," she said reassuringly, "wondering if all will go well today, you know, with Michelle and all."

Actually I wasn't the least bit worried whether or not something would go terribly wrong. The only thing keeping me awake all night were my own thoughts—or doubts—that we had done the right thing. What kind of a life is my child going to have? How can I prepare her for the teasing and taunting she was sure to receive for having two gay dads? Will she resent me? Will she hate me? Will she be happy? How are we going to tell her how she came to be? Will she love Michelle more than me? Those were just some—just some—of the questions, doubts, and thoughts going through my mind. Well, and whether David was going to be able to go with us.

My parents arrived the day before, and I could tell that Mom was worried about us. She did her best to not show it, but I could tell she was worried that everything would turn out okay and that David and I weren't about to have our hopes and dreams dashed. Her question to me in the kitchen that morning reinforced my suspicion. After chugging down two cups of coffee, David finally woke up. "You'll get on the plane dead or alive," I said, "as I don't think I can do this alone. So, you have two choices: either die on that airplane at forty thousand feet, or I'll put you out of your misery first, and then take your corpse with me."

Did I mention that I was beyond bitchy?

Fifteen minutes before the cab pulled up in front of the house, David decided he could make the flight. My threats had nothing to do with it. I do think it helped that I put enough antidiarrhea stuff in his coffee that he wouldn't poop for a year.

Strangely enough, we didn't talk very much on the flight. David slept while Mom and I made idle chitchat. The strangest part of the flight was that we checked in with an empty car seat. It seemed so huge. I couldn't for the life of me picture a baby filling up the entire seat. I also couldn't for the life of me believe that we were leaving New York as a couple but returning as a family.

Journal Entry, October 2003
"I can't move," Michelle told one of the nurses, who was trying to get her flat on her back. "I just can't." With that Michelle let out a grunt and was told to push again. "I can't wait," Michelle repeated over and over to me, "I can't wait for David."

We landed in Reno on Wednesday, October 1, and made a beeline to the hospital in California. Michelle had been there since six o'clock that morning, so I called her to check in and see how she was doing. She was surprisingly calm and upbeat, although she did say that she didn't have to be there so early in the morning after all. "I could have stayed in bed until at least eight," she said with a sigh. "All I did was sit around for almost two hours this morning waiting." She sounded happy though, if not relieved, to hear that we were on our way.

The day before we left, Michelle called me at work, frantic while standing in line at the car rental agency booth. They weren't going to let her rent the car that I had called and reserved for her, as the name on the registration form didn't match the credit card information I had given them. I tried calling her back but missed her. After a few tense minutes Michelle was finally able to pick up her cell phone.

"I'm standing in the line to take the bus," she said on the verge of tears.

"A bus?" I said in surprise. "Are you sure you can get on a bus?" *Nice,* I thought. *What a lovely thing to say to a woman who is already crying and nine months pregnant.*

"I'll be fine," she said reassuringly. "I'll be fine." One crisis down, one more to go!

An hour or so later the phone rang again at work. It was Michelle. This time she was standing at the check-in counter of the hotel we had booked for her. Once again, her name didn't match the credit card information that I had given them and they weren't letting her in the room. I scrambled and faxed a letter along with a copy of my credit card so that Michelle could check in.

What was supposed to have been a simple trip had turned into a nightmare for her. Part of me couldn't believe that she hadn't gotten fed up enough to throw her hands in the air and head on home. She had spent the entire week by herself—away from her family—walking and trying to keep herself busy. I would have gone bonkers. "I thought for sure," Michelle said later on, "that little miss wanted to make her appearance early." Come to find out she had been having horrible contractions anytime she walked for any distance.

After a forty-five-minute drive and checking into our room, we all headed over to the hospital. Michelle was sitting up in bed reading one of her favorite books. She looked up with a smile and a giggle and said, "You guys just missed the doctor. She was here about a half an hour ago or so and broke my water, but other than that there isn't much going on." She certainly didn't look thirty-eight weeks and six days pregnant—let alone just had her water broken. "I'm only about four centimeters dilated," she said, "so we have a long way to go before we make it to ten."

It was just so good to see her. It had been since May that we had seen each other in person, and I couldn't believe how wonderful she looked. I felt terribly guilty that she was there all by herself. It seemed like so much for her to do alone. Having been separated from her family the entire week couldn't have been easy, then the drama of getting from Reno to California, but there she was—sitting up in bed ready to take on the world—despite having contractions every three minutes.

We weren't sure what to do. Michelle was doing all the work; somehow we formed a semicircle with our chairs around her bed. It felt like hours were going by as we sat and stared at her. Every now and then she would let out an "oh," or "ah," maybe even an "ouch," and that was it. Had it been me it would have been like a scene out of *The Exorcist,* complete with spinning heads spewing green stuff. All the while, the look on Michelle's face was priceless.

"Why don't you guys go and get something to eat," she said with a grin, knowing that she was breaking the silence. "You must be tired, and I promise there's nothing going on." We took that hint and ran with it. I wanted David to get back to the hotel anyway, as he still didn't look too well. Before he left, I promised to call him the minute something, anything, started to happen.

Right after Mom and I got back, Michelle was given an epidural—you know—the lovely shot that numbs your entire lower body. "How has everyone been treating you?" I asked when they were done.

"Mike, everyone has been fantastic!" Michelle said, beaming ear to ear. "They all know I'm a surrogate and no one has had anything mean to say. No one has acted weird or anything. I'm shocked and thankful."

The hours passed slowly but surely. Amazingly, Michelle stayed in good spirits and kept breathing through her contractions. I honestly didn't know what to expect. I had heard the horror stories of screaming, yelling, and throwing things during labor and delivery, but I swear you would never know that Michelle was about to give birth. "They don't hurt," she said, while trying to describe the contractions.

"It just feels like a lot of pressure, and they are getting stronger and quicker."

By six o'clock she started feeling the full brunt of them. A nurse confirmed that Michelle was six centimeters dilated and about eighty-percent effaced.

"What does that mean?" I asked the nurse.

"That means things are going along pretty well," the nurse replied, "but we still have a ways to go, so I would suggest getting comfortable."

"Well," Michelle chimed in, "I'm getting more and more uncomfortable with each contraction, so I'd like my epi upped if that's possible?"

I could tell from the tone of her voice that she was starting to get anxious. Several times she had complained of feeling a great deal of pressure during the contractions, but she would have to wait because the anesthesiologist had gone to his son's soccer game and he wasn't due back for at least half an hour. The nurse wanted to check Michelle again, so Mom and I made our way to the other side of the curtain. The very next thing I heard was Michelle yelling, "Mike, call David! Call David now! This baby is coming!"

We scrambled back into the room not knowing what to do or where to go. Mom headed toward Michelle, who was lying on her side, and I bolted to the phone. David picked up after the first ring.

"You better get over here," I said, trying not to sound too panicked.

"I'm on my way," David said. "Everything will be fine."

By now, both Mom and Michelle were sobbing through the latest contraction. I just remember my heart jumping into my mouth. There was no time. The baby was coming and there was no time.

It had been four hours since we arrived, but it was time. Michelle's obstetrician had been paged, and as she walked into the room I switched places with Mom and held Michelle's hand.

"Do I have time to change my shoes?" the doctor joked. "They're new! I'd hate to ruin them!"

"No, doctor!" an excited nurse in the room yelled. "There's no time. Get over here, now!"

Michelle had crowned—meaning they could see the baby's head. Suddenly there was a flurry of activity. Mom was standing about a foot away and sobbing, two nurses had come into the room with a large table covered in blue cloth, and the doctor was getting into position. Everything and everyone was ready, except David.

"I can't move," Michelle told one of the nurses, who was trying to get her flat on her back. "I just can't." With that she let out a grunt and was told to push again.

"I can't wait," she repeated over and over to me.

"Wait for what?" I asked.

"I can't wait for David," she said in between huffs and puffs.

"Just do what you have to do, Michelle," I said, while trying not to look. "He'll be here any second, but do what you have to do."

With that she let out another grunt and pushed again. The next sound we all heard was what sounded like a whoosh and the screams of a newborn baby.

"Congratulations, Daddy!" the doctor said as she held up a squirming and confused newborn baby. "It's a girl!"

My head hit Michelle's chest and we both burst into tears. It was 6:40 p.m., PST. The world stood still. All I could say was "Thank you. Thank you." I just couldn't stop saying thank you. Michelle couldn't stop saying, "No, thank you" in return. We cried, we laughed, and we stared in amazement. The next thing I knew, Lillian Barbara Menichiello was held up in front of me and I cut the cord, crying all the while. Wouldn't you know, at that very same moment a stunned David walked through the door. The anesthesiologist was right behind him.

"That was way too fast. Did I tear?" Michelle asked the doctor.

"No," the doctor said, "she came out so fast you're lucky there aren't skid marks!" We all shared a laugh, and David and I broke down in each other's arms. We were now officially daddies.

"I did it! I really, really did it!" Michelle repeated over and over through tears. "I helped make a family."

"Yes, you did," David said. "You've made our dreams come true, and for that we can't thank you enough."

The next few hours were spent in examination rooms where Lillian was weighed (eight pounds on the nose) and measured (twenty inches long). I couldn't take my eyes off of her. She was absolutely gorgeous, with a full head of blonde hair and sparkling blue eyes. Her handprints and footprints were taken and she took it all in stride. By the time we got back to the room, Michelle was already sitting up in bed eating dinner. We brought Lilly in again for Michelle to see her, now that she was cleaned up and had calmed down.

"She has my nose," Michelle said, "but she has your eyes and your cheeks."

While David and I stood amazed it was Mom's turn to break down and have a moment.

"I can't believe you did this for my son and David, Michelle," Mom started out. "I just can't believe you did this for them, for me, for my family. I'm so happy. I'm so proud. We love you so very much for doing this. I can't thank you enough. All I can say is thank you. Thank you. She's just gorgeous."

It took an hour or so for us all to get even remotely collected before the nurse walked into the private room and announced that both Michelle and Lilly were being released from the hospital the very next morning. Yes, the very next morning! So much for being in there for twenty-four hours and for Michelle getting some much-needed rest.

We ended up booking Michelle an adjoining room at our hotel. Before we left that night, David and I gave Michelle a heart-shaped diamond necklace to show our love and appreciation. "Stop thanking me," she said. "I'm the one who has to thank you guys for choosing me and making my dreams come true."

After staring at Lilly for another hour or so we headed back to the hotel to get some much-needed rest. Michelle asked if she could see Lilly. "Of course," I said. "See her as much as you would like." Before leaving we stopped by the nurse's station to make certain that Michelle could ask for and see Lilly at any time. The next morning at eleven o'clock, Michelle and Lilly were officially discharged.

I can't begin to explain how amazing it was to be sitting in our hotel room that night with David, my mother, my daughter, and our surrogate mother, all celebrating the arrival of a very special little girl. We spent the night in California before heading back toward Reno to see Michelle off. Our pediatrician suggested keeping Lilly put until that coming Sunday at the earliest—and that was three days away.

The next morning we all went to have breakfast at a restaurant right across the parking lot from our hotel. I couldn't take my eyes off of Michelle. Yes, Michelle. I sat there and stared at her in amazement and sheer disbelief for what she had just done two days before. While waitresses busily took orders, Mom, David, and Michelle made small talk, Lilly slept snug as a bug in a rug, and busboys cleared tables, all I could do was sit and wonder. Two days before, the woman sitting across from me gave birth to my daughter. For months she stood by us, supported us, drove me nearly crazy, but never once did she ever doubt that this very day would happen. She never doubted that David and I would have our own family. I couldn't help but wonder what she was thinking.

"Are you okay?" I asked her right before she took a sip of juice.

"Me?" Michelle said, surprised. "Oh, I'm fine. I'm fine."

"What does it feel like?" I asked her. "I mean, what does it feel like right now to be sitting here with us, knowing that you brought her into this world?"

"Well," she said, starting to blush, "actually, it's amazing. I can't believe it. I did it. It's just an amazing feeling."

"Not many women could do what you just did for these guys," my mom chimed in.

"How are you?" I asked again. "I'm just worried that you're okay."

"Don't I seem okay?" Michelle asked. "It's not the same. It's not the same feeling, I mean, the feeling that I had with my own children. I knew all along that this little one was going to go home with you guys. I've had months to get ready for it. I'm okay. I knew what I was getting into. I gave it a lot of thought. I mean, look at you guys. You are both beaming. You look really, really, tired, but you're beaming. She's beautiful. I made it happen. I did it. I really, really, did it."

"She'll know you one day, you know?" I said. "I promise you that."

"I know, Mike," Michelle said with a smile. "I did this for myself as much as I did it for you guys. I've never done something so amazing. Who would have thought that?"

"Any regrets?" I asked. "Please tell me if you ever have any regrets."

"Nope, none," she said emphatically. "None at all. Look at her. She's gorgeous. You're happy and I'm happy; that's all that matters."

That afternoon we drove to Reno with Mom and Michelle sitting in the backseat with Lilly in her new car seat. I kept looking in the rearview mirror, watching Michelle beaming with pride. That afternoon, before we knew it, we were walking her to the gate at the airport. After long hugs and fawning over Lilly, we watched Michelle walk down the aisle toward the security checkpoint. We didn't say goodbye, just, "Talk to you tonight." I stood there and watched Michelle slowly make her way through security and then disappear into the crowd. It was a strange moment. After all we had been through, Michelle was walking away. How do you experience such an incredible journey with someone and then just watch as she walks away? A monumental thing had just happened, and it seemed as though there should be some spectacular ending. There weren't any lights or cameras or fireworks, just three grateful people with tears rolling down their cheeks holding a two-day-old baby watching the woman who made it all happen walking away. A life-altering event had just taken place, but you would have never known it.

I held it all inside until we had made it back to the parking garage. Just as I closed the tailgate on the truck Mom asked me what was wrong. I simply could not believe what Michelle had just done.

"She's just given birth to her own daughter, Mom," I said while collapsing in her arms. "She just handed me my daughter and we just said good-bye. She did it for us. I can't believe she did this for us and she walked away alone. I just hope she's okay, that's all. I just hope to God that she's going to be okay."

"She did it because she wanted to do it, Mike," my mom said, trying to reassure me.

"What's the matter?" David asked as he made his way toward the back of the truck.

"I just don't know how she could do something like this for us. I mean, look at her. Look at Lilly. She's gorgeous. She's here. She's ours. She's our daughter and she wouldn't be here if it weren't for Michelle."

Part of me couldn't believe that I was now a father and the other part couldn't believe that I wasn't going to see my child's birth mother for what would probably be a very long time. I just lost it. Thank God Mom and David were both there to pick up the pieces. All the worrying—the waiting—the wondering—the anger—the joy—the frustration—the amazement—all came out in a garage at Reno-Tahoe International Airport. I don't know how Michelle did what she did. I probably never will be able to understand it. How do you give a couple the gift of life and expect nothing, or little, in return? How do you trust that they will raise a child that is part of you? How do you give so much of yourself? They are questions that only Michelle can answer. The four of us—three sobbing all the way—started driving toward the Hilton in downtown Reno, where we thought we could find a room for two nights. We had no such luck.

Journal Entry, October 2003
It's three o'clock in the morning and I'm wide awake. Mom and David are sound asleep and I just finished giving Lilly her bottle filled with formula and changing her hundredth dirty diaper of the day. How incredible is this—how absolutely incredible. She's so tiny, so perfect. Her tiny little hands are clenched in tight little fists. I wonder what she sees. Will she be happy? All I can think of, and it's going over and over in my head, is that song from a Doris Day television show, "Que Sera, Sera." You know the song? "When I was just a little girl, I asked my mother, 'What will I be? Will I be happy? Will I be rich?' Here's what she said to me: 'Que sera, sera, whatever will be, will be.'"

Every hotel in Reno was booked solid for the entire weekend. Luckily, David called our beloved Circus Circus on a whim. Believe it or not, they had a room. The irony of it all was that it was at Circus Circus nine months ago when Michelle felt the telltale ache of ovulation. As we stood in the hotel lobby waiting to register, we knew that we had come full circle. We were right back at the very same place where Lilly had been conceived. What a sight that had to have been. Who would have thought that they would see two dads and a grandmother holding a newborn baby waiting in line to check into their hotel room at a casino in Reno Nevada? But there we stood.

Picture this: three adults and a three-day-old baby in the last vacant hotel room in all of Reno, with two double beds. That should sum things up. We took turns feeding and changing Lilly while trying to grab some much-needed sleep in between. Mom was amazing, even making sure Lilly got some indirect sunlight on and off during the day, since she was slightly jaundiced. None of us could believe that we were actually there. None of us could believe that we were actually three thousand miles away from home taking care of a newborn baby. "How old is she?" one of the waitresses asked while we were at dinner one night. "Well, she's three days old," my mother said. "Three weeks?" the dumbfounded waitress asked. "No," Mom said, "just three days."

Michelle called later that night to let us know that she had made it home safe and sound. She seemed fine and sounded happy to be back with her husband and her kids. I just remember reminding her to drop off the film in her camera to get it developed. She had taken some pictures of Lilly in our hotel room, wearing an outfit that her daughter had bought for her. We both held back tears. Neither one of us wanted to upset the other. "Stop asking me if I'm okay," she said with her trademark giggle. "I'm fine. I'm truly fine. The kids are so excited that I'm back. I'm fine. I'm tired and want to sleep for a week, but trust me, I'm fine."

Finally, Sunday came and we were on our way home.

"Where's her mother?" the flight attendant asked the three of us. Come to find out, we had been the talk of the entire crew that day. Speculation among the flight attendants had it that Mom was the birth mother and David and I were the adoptive parents. Apparently, we were the talk of the cabin. Mom was flattered, of course. David wanted to know why they thought we were gay. She had actually been the fifth person to ask us that very same question as we made our way back to New York. The first person to ask was the security guard at the airport. After making small talk and ogling Lilly for a little bit she finally looked up sheepishly and asked if the mother was in the rest room. "She's back home in Arizona," I would say to everyone and anyone that asked. "Lilly's surrogate mom is probably home in Arizona by now." No one batted an eye. Sure, you would get the, "Oh," followed of course by the longer, "Oh, I see," as the reality of what I had said started to settle in. I had gotten used to saying it. I had also started getting used to the puzzled looks on their faces.

The first four days weren't easy, that's for sure. All of us were still reeling from the flight out and the change in time zones, and between the four of us I think we managed to get an average of two or three hours of sleep a night. I was in rare form. I was tired, irritable, cranky, and sleep deprived. Not a pretty sight. Not a pretty sight at all. As a matter of fact, for weeks afterward I apologized profusely to both my mother and David for how I had behaved at times. At one point I thought David and I were going to get into a full-blown catfight right smack in the middle of an airport. You know how when you're arguing with someone in a public place you start out gritting your teeth and mumbling, but you get so carried away and lose track of where you actually are and before you know it you have an audience? Yeah, I know that feeling all too well. Thankfully, Lilly slept through most of it. I don't remember exactly what we were fighting about, but I think it had something to do with what we were going to eat for lunch, where we were getting it, and who was going to walk over and get it. To say that I was stressed out, scared out of my mind, and tired would be an understatement. The most stressful part, for some reason, was that I was afraid Lilly would throw an absolute fit of crying in the middle of the airport. What I should have been afraid of was David booking me a flight to another country. At one point, I actually told David to shut up. Many things can be said to make someone you love blow a gasket. Telling them to shut up is one of them. David and I definitely had some adjusting to do. A few short hours later the plane finally landed in New York City and we were on our way home. I never thought I would be so happy to set eyes on LaGuardia Airport.

9

Life with Lilly

Journal Entry, November 2003
I'm absolutely exhausted. Thrilled, but exhausted. I'm also a lit-
tle scared. Lilly has been crying nonstop for two hours. I'm just
about ready to pull every last hair right out of my head. I love
her madly, but if she doesn't stop crying I'm going to cry and
then all hell is going to break loose. I can't believe I'm actually
thinking this, but I can't wait until she can talk. At least then she
can tell me what's wrong. The only problem is I don't think
she'll stop talking when she starts. If she's anything like her
daddy, that is.

The day after getting back to New York City we all headed upstate
so the rest of my family could meet the latest addition. After spending
a week getting some much-needed sleep, the three of us were on our
own and we headed back home.

"You know something," David said in the car, "it's never going to
be just you and me anymore. It's now going to be you, me, and Lilly."
No more last-minute movies on the weekends. No more quick trips
to the store. No more grocery shopping just for two. It had finally
started to settle in that the two of us had now officially become the
three of us.

I still couldn't believe how tiny she was. Everything was all in
place—right where it should be—but it was all in highly detailed
miniature. She seemed so fragile, but Michelle kept reminding us just
how flexible or "rubbery" babies really were. I also learned how for-
giving they could be. I was scared to death of the umbilical cord
stump. Every day it had to be cleaned, and I dreaded doing it. Lilly,
however, didn't have a clue, or if she did she certainly didn't seem to
show it.

David was able to stay home with us for a few days before return-ing to work, but then I was on my own. "It's just you and me now, kid," I said, looking at Lilly smiling. "You're stuck with me now." I had taken a three-month leave of absence from work and I knew after the first week that it was all going to go by much too quickly.

It took a few days and my fears started to calm down. I somehow—slowly but surely—managed to settle in and even started to form some semblance of a daily routine. However, it didn't take long for me to realize that Lilly didn't have need for any kind or type of rou-tine. Actually the first few weeks weren't all that bad. Mom kept tell-ing me beforehand that it didn't take a brain surgeon to care for an in-fant. "They let you know when they want something, Mike," she said one night on the telephone. "Believe me, they will let you know. It's either they are hungry, tired, or need to be changed."

I was scared to death that I'd screw something up. Changing dia-pers didn't faze me. A couple of times, though, we had some projec-tile poop, but thankfully moments like those were pretty few and far between.

The first few weeks she slept; and I mean slept. Sometimes she'd sleep up to fourteen hours a day, waking only to eat; and I mean eat. Despite the lack of sleep, I seemed to adjust well to taking care of her. If only that feeling would have lasted. At about the sixth week, the screaming began; and I mean screaming. The kind of screaming that would ring in my ears for hours afterward. "Why is she screaming?" I asked David one morning around one o'clock. "She's been screaming for two hours and I can't get her to stop." There were times that we thought the screaming would never end. It took me a few days of try-ing everything and anything that I could think of to make it stop, be-fore breaking down and sounding a general alarm. No, make that a five alarm. E-mails and phone calls went out to family and friends—with children or without—searching for answers. They were surpris-ingly short and sweet, some of them consisting of one single word that seemed to sum it all up: "HELP!"

However, the replies surprised me more than the screaming. Some suggested cure-alls that had worked for them in the past, like putting the baby in the car seat and driving around for hours at a time. My nerves couldn't handle that. The last thing I wanted to do with a screaming baby was wrap her up, bundle her in the car seat, then drive around while she screamed her fool head off. Others said to try putting her on top of the clothes dryer while it was running. Supposedly the sound and motion often worked as some form of bizarre comfort. We have a stackable washer and dryer, though, so that was out of the question.

I would have tried almost anything to make it stop. I even remember switching her formula three times, including doing it once without telling the doctor. That, needless to say, didn't go over very well at all. One friend and fellow parent actually had a name for what we were enduring. It was the dreaded "colic." "You have one heck of a colicky baby," a friend wrote in an e-mail. "I wish you luck, patience, and some new ear drums." It was my ultimate worst fear. I remembered when my sister Debbie had my niece and nephew—both of them had the dreaded colic. I would last about fifteen minutes in her house and then would run like a girly man. I searched online for remedies and found a product called "gripe water." It was only sold in ten-ounce bottles, but before all was said and done, I think we ended up going through gallons of it. Finally, I broke down and made another appointment with our pediatrician. It turned out to be an interesting appointment, to say the least. From our very first visit to her office, I had a gut feeling that she wasn't so keen on the idea of two gay dads caring for a newborn baby. The look of puzzlement on her face left me constantly wondering if she was thinking, "What could two men possibly know about taking care of a newborn baby?" She never said anything overt, but the undertones were there. At our appointment I think she was more shocked than anything.

"Well, Mike," she said, "babies cry, you know."

"Yes," I said with my hands on my hips. "I know they cry, but this isn't what I consider crying."

"Well, you know," she continued, trying to talk louder than the screaming, "you don't have to give her food every time she cries."

Why didn't I think of that? No, next time I'll just break out in song and dance. Yeah, that's it. That will make her stop.

"Well," I asked with my hands still on my hips, "this is more like screaming to me, not crying. I can barely hear a word you're saying to me right now. Is this what you call crying?" The doctor just stood there in disbelief. "If this is Lilly crying," I threw in for added measure, "I don't even want to be in the same state as her when she actually lets out a scream."

There we stood—two grown adults—trying to talk over the screams. It's like people who talk during a movie. They have to talk louder to hear themselves over the movie. Don't you just hate that?

"This isn't crying," I repeated, really starting to lose my patience. "This is screaming, and I can't hear a word you're saying to me!"

That's about how the entire appointment came and went. I somehow managed to tell her that I was flat-out scared. Something seemed to be wrong with Lilly and I was powerless to do anything about it. Was she in pain? Was she hurting?

"So is this colic?" I managed to ask.

"It's only considered colic if it's incessant crying that lasts for several hours a day, sometimes upwards of four hours at a time," she said firmly, "and it has to last for at least three weeks."

"No," I said, "that's not colic. That's what I'm going to end up being like if this screaming doesn't stop soon. I'm the one who's going to be screaming several hours a day for several weeks in a padded cell."

That's when it finally dawned on me that no one really knows what colic is, how babies get it, or what to do to help them get over it. Well, other than my favorite phrase, "Oh, they'll grow out of it. It generally only lasts until they are six months old." In six months I would be locked away somewhere in a lovely, white, form-fitting suit babbling to myself; then I wouldn't care about colic.

All I wanted were answers, but I ended up coming home with more of a headache than before. I did find out that Lilly didn't have colic, she was just crying. Yeah, right. Speaking of crying, it's funny, but people kept telling me that we would get to know her cries. There would be a certain cry if she was hungry and another if she was wet and needed a diaper change. A different cry would be heard if she was frustrated, had a gas bubble, needed to be burped, or was bored. And cry she did. It took about two weeks, and then one morning I realized that she made a little hiccup sound at the end of her cry that went away the moment she was fed. It was like finding the Holy Grail. That discovery, combined with her nightly cocktail of formula, antigas drops, and gripe water, soothed our weary ears. The best part was that it allowed Lilly to actually get some rest. I had learned one of her cries and I would learn many more during the first month that we were home. Lilly and I were now officially communicating with each other.

Isn't communication a wonderful thing? In a few weeks, the scream-ing stopped as suddenly as it had begun.

Journal Entry, December 2003
If David tells me one more time that some nurse at work has told him that I should sleep when Lilly sleeps I'm going to lose it. I already feel like I'm one can short of a six-pack, and all I keep hearing from him is that I should be sleeping when she's sleep-ing. Okay, Lilly sleeps about fourteen hours a day. If I were get-ting that much sleep I would be in a coma. Sleep when she sleeps? I wish. By the time I give her some formula, burp her, change her, put her back down to sleep, clean the bottle, and make formula, she's awake again! How the heck am I supposed to sleep when she sleeps?

Michelle and I exchanged e-mails almost every week. She was do-ing really well. I kept asking her if she was okay. I couldn't help but wonder if she had any regrets or mixed feelings about what she had done for us. Every time the response was the same: "I have no re-grets," she would write. "I'm so proud of what I've done and have ab-solutely no regrets." Every week like clockwork I would take Lilly's photo and send it off to everyone and anyone who was unfortunate enough to be in my address book. "She looks so much like you, Mike," Michelle wrote one week. "She's your clone." I also started a weekly ritual of giving Lilly one kiss on the forehead for every week since her birthday.

The days turned into weeks and the weeks turned into months. Be-fore I knew it, eight weeks had gone by, and it was time to start check-ing into full-time day care. A colleague of David's at work suggested that we look into the day care center where she had been taking her son. Within a week we had an appointment and met with the owner. It didn't take long for us to decide that it would be a great place for Lilly to spend her day. The owner put us right at ease by sharing with us that her son was gay and that they would take care of Lilly very well. "No one will have a problem with you here," she said firmly, "and if they do, it won't be your problem, it will be theirs—as they'll be look-ing for another job." We both knew that she meant what she said.

I was absolutely, unequivocally, dreading the first morning of day care and found myself stalling to leave the house. First, I wasn't thrilled about going back to work, and second, I had just spent three solid months with Lilly. I would miss her terribly. We both cried all the way there, but once downstairs in the playroom we were both fine. Carla, one of the day care workers, had taken an immediate liking to Lilly, and the minute Lilly saw her she let out a huge smile. I knew she was going to be in very good hands.

We fell into a daily routine of sorts. Mornings were like being a contestant on the old game show *Beat the Clock.* We would get up at six-thirty, wake up Lilly, and get her changed, fed, burped, and happy. Then I would shower, shave, feed the dog and cats, warm up the car, get Lilly in her coat, let the dog out for one last pee if it was raining, and then bolt to day care. Nights were no different. Race home, throw something on for dinner, get Lilly changed, fed, burped, and in her bouncy seat to entertain herself while we got changed, ate, and burped. Life was going pretty well. Then, in February, David took Lilly for what was supposed to be a routine doctor's appointment. Later that afternoon he called me at work and left a message asking me to call him right back. I knew something was wrong.

"Lilly didn't pass her eye exam," David said, trying not to scare the hell out of me. "The doctor did the test three times and on one out of the three she thought she saw something. So she's sending us to a specialist just to make sure."

Of course I asked him what she saw.

"She saw a white rim around her retina," David explained, "and it's something that she shouldn't see."

For some reason I was very positive and upbeat about the whole thing. That is, until I got home that night and David started doing research on the Internet. At one point, I went downstairs to get Lilly's bottle ready. When I came back upstairs David was lying in bed with her and he was obviously very upset.

"What's the matter?" I asked him. "Why are you crying?" David got up from bed and went over to the computer.

"The anomaly that she saw this afternoon," he said, "is one of three things."

"Okay," I said. "Well, it can't be all that bad, is it?"

"Well," David said before starting to cry again, "it's nothing, or the white rim around the retina could mean that Lilly is developing an astigmatism, which is highly unlikely, or that a tumor has developed behind her eye."

"Did you say a tumor? How can that be?" I asked in shock.

"Not just a tumor," David said through tears. "It could be a cancerous tumor."

I didn't have to hear anything else before I was on my knees. At first I was completely shocked. Then, I was angry. Then fear settled in. "Oh God," I said, "if anything happens to her, I swear to God if anything happens to her I will kill myself. I can't watch her go through something like that. I can't." Lilly was lying in bed staring up at me, probably wondering what in the world her weirdo father was doing now.

"It looks like it's treatable," David said. "They would have to do chemo and radiation therapy, so at least it seems like it's treatable, if that's what it is."

"What if that doesn't work?" I asked.

David went on to explain that if all else failed they would actually remove the entire eye. I couldn't believe what I had just heard, nor could I believe David's reaction. Normally he's calm, cool, and collected, but this time he was shaken—visibly shaken. It's not that often that I see David so shaken up. He had made a doctor's appointment with a pediatric ophthalmologist for that coming Friday. I begged him to do whatever he could at work the next day to make the appointment sooner. I swear that entire night we held Lilly, cried, sobbed, and prayed to God that she would be okay. I kept trying to tell myself that it was probably nothing. It had to be a false positive. It just didn't make sense. The next morning David called from work saying that a doctor at the hospital had pulled some strings and gotten Lilly an appointment for that very same afternoon. Four hours later David called to let me know that she was given a clean bill of health. The anomaly was just that. It was a total fluke.

I've never felt so relieved in my entire life. "Get used to it," a fellow parent at work said to me after I told her the news. "It's all part of being a parent. There will be many more times when you'll have the hell scared out of you. It's par for the course."

"So," my mom started to ask with a grin, "what is she going to call you guys? I mean, are you going to be Dad and Daddy, or Dad and Papa? What is she going to call you, or what are you going to call yourselves?"

Good question, Mom, good question. I had started to call David "Papa" in the airport, but it didn't take him long to let me know that he wasn't so fond of that title. "Can't we come up with something else?"

he asked. "Papa makes me sound like I'm a hundred years old or something." Okay.

"But," I said, "if we're both Dad isn't that going to be confusing?" Honestly, we never really settled on anything other than Dad and Daddy. I'm sure in a few years Lilly will have plenty of names for us.

"What about Michelle?" Mom then asked. "What will she be called?" Well, wasn't Mom full of interesting, provocative questions?

"I really don't want to come up with a title or a label for her," I said, off the top of my head. "I mean, I don't want Lilly to feel that she has to call Michelle anything in particular. To me, Michelle is Lilly's mother. Whether she's called mother, or birth mother, or Mom, I'll leave up to Lilly."

> *Journal Entry, March 2004*
> *What a day! I still can't believe it myself, but David and I are officially married! David, me, and Lilly stood in front of a minister this morning in New Paltz, New York, and exchanged our vows after sixteen years. What an amazing day, and what an amazing feeling.*

Our phone rang on a Thursday evening at nine-thirty. My first thought when the phone rang was that it was going to wake up a sleeping Lilly. She had just fallen asleep while lying over my shoulder, having just polished off her final bottle of the night. It's the most amazing feeling in the world, by they way, to have a baby fall asleep on your shoulder. To have her so close, and to know it won't be long before she'll be too big to do it makes it all the more special. David bolted for the phone—he always does, because our phone rings louder than Big Ben. I can't for the life of me figure out how to turn it down—it's new, and new technology and I just don't get along.

"It's someone calling from New Paltz," David said as he turned to me while muffling the phone, "and they want to know if we can get married this weekend?"

"This weekend! As in this coming weekend?" I asked in disbelief. "That's nuts!" I continued to go off on a minitirade about timing, and poor timing, and how can we get married with one day's notice—David had long since resumed his conversation. All I could see at that point was the back of his head bobbing and his hand up in the air motioning me to clam up.

"I think we can make it," David said without hesitation. "Can't we?" he finally turned to me and asked. A wedding, after all wouldn't be all that much of a wedding without one of the husbands-to-be.

"Um, sure," I said, rolling my eyes, "but I don't know how we're going to do all of this. I mean we don't have rings and we don't even have witnesses. And another thing, you have to work Friday night—remember? You're supposed to be on call Friday night. Then, there's Mom and Dad. They are going to kill us. There's no way they can make it here from Florida in one day. Mom is going to completely freak out when she hears this one. Plus, we have nothing to wear. I don't think I can fit into any of the suits we have. I don't even know where they are. How far is New Paltz from here anyway? It's like four hours away or something, isn't it? How are we going to get there? How are we going to do this all in one day? Don't you have to work? What about Lilly? What am I supposed to do, put her in a baggie from the grocery store? We don't have a dress for her. I don't have anything for her to wear and she's not wearing shoes yet. She's going to at least need a dress. What about rings? We don't have rings, you know. Can we take her there with no shoes on? Are you listening to me? David? David?"

I don't think he had heard one-tenth of my tirade. He was in what I call his "ignore mode." Lilly was still asleep, thankfully. I don't know why I get that way when I'm stressed. I really don't. It's like all these thoughts come to me all at once and I know David isn't listening to one single word of it. He tunes out after the first syllable. But alas, they would both hear it over and over and over again between then and Friday. The funny part, to me anyway, was that ever since I had called a month before and added our names to the waiting list, David had started obsessing about our rings. Every night without fail he would present me with print-outs from the computer that featured a lovely assortment of shapes, sizes, and styles of rings. He would then proceed to ask me if I liked each and every one of them. Would they be gold? Platinum? What about white gold with platinum edges? How does yellow gold look with platinum edges? What size? Do you like 14-karat gold or 18-karat gold? Do you like this one? Why not? What about this one? No? Why? I like it. Do you like it? Oh wait, forget about platinum, it's way too expensive. He's every bit as bad as I am!

David found our suits and left them hanging in the bedroom to air out. I raced over to the store and bought Lilly the most beautiful pink linen dress, with four tiny pink bows down the front, sleeveless of course, very "Jackie O," without the pillbox hat. Plus, someone had given us tights as a gift at one of our baby showers, so her feet wouldn't be hanging out. Friday night, David raced over to the jewelers and bought our rings. They even stretched them for us, as they didn't have them in our sizes. We called our close friends Mary and Alyce and sprang the news on them. We also asked if they would be our witnesses. The main issue what that on the very same night as our newly arranged wedding day, they had planned an annual event known as the Pajama Bowl-a-Rama. It would be our first year participating, and it was all set, complete with twenty or so people signed up to attend, for Saturday evening at six-thirty. Great timing. Nevertheless, Mary and Alyce said they'd love to be there with us and wouldn't miss it for the world. We made our plans to be on the road by eight-thirty Saturday morning. New Paltz was about two hours away, and we had to be there by ten o'clock. Not the easiest thing in the world to do when you're working with a six-month-old. We pulled into the bed-and-breakfast where the ceremonies were taking place at ten-thirty, and all of us signed the paperwork to get married. Yes, all of us. Come to find out there were one or two no-shows, so Mary and Alyce joined in—after I opened my yap—and walked down the aisle for the second time. They had had a civil union ceremony in Provincetown several years back.

I wasn't feeling nervous or anxious until just before we pulled into the B&B. Then, the butterflies hit. Nearly 200 people were milling around, including a TV news crew from Plattsburgh. We signed in, met our minister briefly, and then immediately tried to find a quiet place to feed Lilly. At almost one-thirty Saturday afternoon David and I said our official "I dos" and "I wills." It was, without a doubt, the second most wonderful moment in my lifetime. Whether it was an official "marriage" or not, it felt so powerful to be standing before God and have our relationship blessed. It was even more meaningful holding Lilly throughout the ceremony—giggling and cooing all the way through.

"She stole the show," our minister said later. I started crying moments before we hit the altar. I looked up at David moments before the ceremony started and he, too, was teary eyed. So where was our reception, you're wondering? Well, it was at the Burger King drive-through in New Paltz, thank you. Our honeymoon? Well, we spent that at a bowling alley back on Long Island. David actually bowled a decent game or two while wearing his boxer shorts. I sat out the event and tended to Lilly while eating nachos and pizza. It wasn't exactly the wedding of our dreams—no seaside service overlooking the cliffs of Monterey, no limousine to whisk us off to Hawaii. Nope. Just french fries and bowling. However, it was our wedding nonetheless. It was our day. Sixteen years in the making. It's a day that we'll never forget.

Three days later, as promised, the minister sent us a copy of the newspaper article that appeared in Sunday's newspaper following our ceremony. A newspaper reporter and photographer had followed her to New Paltz to document her experience. There we were, the three of us, with our picture right smack on the front page of the paper, in a photograph taken moments before we exchanged our vows. Our stepping forward and being among the first gay couples to get married will hopefully mean something to Lilly someday. Hopefully, by doing so, people will start to see that we're just like everyone else. We go to work, pay our bills, and try to live, just like everyone else.

Life with Lilly has been more incredible than I ever imagined it would be. One of the most amazing things is the change in David. He's wonderful with her, and I'm seeing a side of him that I've never seen before. It's truly amazing. I had often worried if he would be okay with Lilly, not having a biological relationship to her, but my worries were unfounded. In fact, I don't think it's ever even crossed his mind. Despite his work schedule and crazy, long hours David still takes what he calls a "Lilly Day" regularly, where instead of taking the day off to rest, "I spend it with my daughter," as he says. It's just amazing to see.

I've caught myself several times leaning over the railing on Lilly's crib watching her sleep or play. It's hard not to stare at her. Watching her is like holding a moonbeam in the palm of my hand. It's fascinating, exciting, and it feels like I'm watching a miracle occur right before my eyes. She is our love and our joy, with her infectious giggle and her totally pinchable cheeks. Mom keeps saying, "She's such a happy baby."

I can't wait for the day when she's old enough to meet Michelle. I can't help but wonder what it will be like for her to finally meet and know the woman who brought her into this world. Michelle is one of the most remarkable women I've ever had the privilege to know. It's funny, because I think of myself as being a good person, but I could never do what Michelle did for us. It was such a completely selfless act. Some may say that she was compensated for it, and that is her thanks. I think Michelle was compensated in a much deeper and much more meaningful way. I think it really was something that Michelle had always dreamed of doing. She pulled up the courage to do it from deep within her. I will never forget looking into her eyes the moment after Lilly was born. Her eyes were filled with joy, wonder, amazement, and pride. Many in the surrogacy community believe as we do, that surrogates are angels. Several days after Lilly was born, Michelle posted her birth story on a popular surrogacy Web site and right next to her name appeared a tiny little angel with wings. Michelle had earned her wings.

One weekend afternoon in early March, Michelle and I bumped into each other online. Through instant messages we quickly caught up with each other and exchanged new phone numbers. She and her family had moved again, started new jobs, and the kids had started school. Believe it or not, the subject of us working together again came up. I had forgotten that shortly after Lilly was born, David asked Michelle if she would even remotely consider doing it again. "I'd definitely think about it," Michelle said without hesitation. "Sure, I'd think about it."

Michelle hadn't forgotten that conversation, much to our relief. She had been talking with another couple about the possibility of helping them become parents, but wanted to ask for our "permission," as she called it. "I want to help you guys again," she had said in a previous e-mail, "so if I'm working with another couple I want to be able to tell them that I can help them up until a certain date, but I don't want it to interfere with helping you guys again. I love you guys."

After we talked, something dawned on me and I didn't like the feeling that I was left with. If Michelle did decide to work with another couple and it was another traditional surrogacy that would mean Lilly would have another sibling, in a third family. It started raising all sorts of issues and questions for me. After all, Michelle's very own son and daughter are Lilly's half-brother and half-sister. Someday she will know that and hopefully accept it. Knowing when and how to tell her wasn't something that I had stopped to think about. Then the thought crossed my mind that if Michelle continued to be a traditional surrogate for other couples, let's say even two more couples, that would mean that Lilly would have half-brothers and half-sisters being raised by different families scattered across the country. Would she know them all? Is that okay? How would Lilly feel about that? What if the other couples didn't want their children to know that they had other siblings because of surrogacy? They are all questions that I can't answer. I wish I could. I asked Michelle what she thought and she said, "I honestly don't know, Mike. I hadn't thought of it that way before." Then, I posted the question online and asked traditional surrogates and intended parents alike if they planned to tell their children that they had other siblings via surrogacy. The response was overwhelmingly positive. Most responded that they would tell their children about other siblings they had as a result of a surrogacy.

I still don't know the answer and neither, for that matter, does David. What I do know is that we've made plans to start having our second child with Michelle in early winter. The news has surprised a lot of people, although I'm not sure why. I can't wait to get started. As for Michelle, she and the other couple ended up parting ways. "I'm going to take some time for myself this spring and summer," she said, "and get ready for the fall when we work together again." I was very relieved, and the subject of Michelle doing another surrogacy, for a different couple, hasn't come up again.

Sometimes I wish that I could look into a crystal ball and see what Lilly's life will be like. What pains me the most is that I know she will take more than her fair share of taunting and teasing. It's not that I don't feel as though I have a right to have children, being gay, it's that I still know she'll face discrimination and prejudice throughout her life because of me—because of something that I wanted, and that I did.

As for David, me, and Lilly, David is now officially done with both medical school and his residency. He's working at a local hospital and, despite an oftentimes grueling schedule, he seems to be happy and settling in. It's amazing to see him spread his wings and soar. It's fun to hear him talk about our "sibling project" this fall with Michelle. Neither of us can wait to see her again and for her to see Lilly. It's been two years since we've seen her, and it's time for a long-overdue visit.

As for me, I left the field of television and I'm working toward my MS in mental health counseling. I'm not 100 percent certain what field I'll eventually end up counseling in, but the whole issue of raising Lilly in a nontraditional family has left me eager to learn much more about it and share what I learn with others. What's it like being a dad? It's exhilarating, tough, joyous, relentless, overwhelming, amazing, scary, and fun all rolled into one. The toughest challenges so far have been dealing with feelings of guilt over going back to school and not being home every night with David and Lilly and watching her grow more and more independent. Lilly is a strong-willed, independent person with an infectious giggle and a smile that knocks your socks off. I've learned so much from her. Mostly I've learned to honor, and celebrate, her spirit, her independence, and her individuality.

Life should be very interesting the next few months and years. However, that's a whole other story and maybe a whole other book. Right now, we're just trying to cherish every single moment of our life with Lilly. We are so incredibly blessed.

Index

Wages, 36
Weight, 27
White blood cells
    first appearance of, 60-62
    not completely gone, 67

Xbox, 49

Order a copy of this book with this form or online at:
http://www.haworthpress.com/store/product.asp?sku=5520

A GAY COUPLE'S JOURNEY THROUGH SURROGACY
Intended Fathers

_____in hardbound at $29.95 (ISBN-13: 978-0-7890-2819-8; ISBN-10: 0-7890-2819-0)

_____in softbound at $14.95 (ISBN-13: 978-0-7890-2820-4; ISBN-10: 0-7890-2820-4)

Or order online and use special offer code HEC25 in the shopping cart.

COST OF BOOKS_____

☐ **BILL ME LATER:** (Bill-me option is good on US/Canada/Mexico orders only; not good to jobbers, wholesalers, or subscription agencies.)

☐ Check here if billing address is different from shipping address and attach purchase order and billing address information.

POSTAGE & HANDLING_____
(US: $4.00 for first book & $1.50 for each additional book)
(Outside US: $5.00 for first book & $2.00 for each additional book)

Signature_____

SUBTOTAL_____

☐ **PAYMENT ENCLOSED:** $_____

IN CANADA: ADD 7% GST_____

☐ **PLEASE CHARGE TO MY CREDIT CARD.**

STATE TAX_____
(NJ, NY, OH, MN, CA, IL, IN, PA, & SD residents, add appropriate local sales tax)

☐ Visa ☐ MasterCard ☐ AmEx ☐ Discover
☐ Diner's Club ☐ Eurocard ☐ JCB

Account # _____

FINAL TOTAL_____
(If paying in Canadian funds, convert using the current exchange rate, UNESCO coupons welcome)

Exp. Date_____

Signature_____

Prices in US dollars and subject to change without notice.

NAME_____

INSTITUTION_____

ADDRESS_____

CITY_____

STATE/ZIP_____

COUNTRY_____ COUNTY (NY residents only)_____

TEL_____ FAX_____

E-MAIL_____

May we use your e-mail address for confirmations and other types of information? ☐ Yes ☐ No
We appreciate receiving your e-mail address and fax number. Haworth would like to e-mail or fax special discount offers to you, as a preferred customer. **We will never share, rent, or exchange your e-mail address or fax number.** We regard such actions as an invasion of your privacy.

Order From Your Local Bookstore or Directly From
The Haworth Press, Inc.
10 Alice Street, Binghamton, New York 13904-1580 • USA
TELEPHONE: 1-800-HAWORTH (1-800-429-6784) / Outside US/Canada: (607) 722-5857
FAX: 1-800-895-0582 / Outside US/Canada: (607) 771-0012
E-mail to: orders@haworthpress.com

For orders outside US and Canada, you may wish to order through your local
sales representative, distributor, or bookseller.
For information, see http://haworthpress.com/distributors

(Discounts are available for individual orders in US and Canada only, not booksellers/distributors.)

PLEASE PHOTOCOPY THIS FORM FOR YOUR PERSONAL USE.
http://www.HaworthPress.com   BOF06